Fast Break Basketball

fundamentals and fine points

John B. McLendon, Jr.

Head Basketball Coach
Kentucky State College

West Nyack, N. Y.
PARKER PUBLISHING COMPANY, INC.

PRINTED IN THE UNITED STATES OF AMERICA

30765—BC

Fast Break Basketball

fundamentals

and

fine points

Nils Desparandum

Nils Desparandum, words I always heed;
My inspiration, prayer, and creed;
Life's storms cannot my aspirations dim
For these are words I hear from Him.

ACKNOWLEDGEMENTS

Words are difficult to find and even more difficult to organize when one tries to give adequate credit to those who have been helpful. However, there are certain individuals in the athletic and physical education profession whom I must acknowledge because they have been most responsible for my introduction to the fundamentals and philosophy of basketball. I refer to the late P. L. Jacobs, my junior high school coach, A. T. Edwards, senior high coach, Beltron Orme, my junior college coach, the late Dr. James A. Naismith, inventor of the game of basketball who was my adviser for three years at Kansas University and Dr. W. F. Burghardt whom I assisted while beginning my college career at North Carolina College. Of course, there are others actively and directly responsible for the good years I have enjoyed; the fair, good, and great basketball players who have believed in the Fast Break doctrine and my assistants at various times, Floyd Brown, Dr. L. T. Walker, Dick Mack and Harold Hunter. In each of these men there was the wholehearted loyalty and ever-eager industriousness which made my job always pleasant and rewarding.

I must add that I am thankful to my mother who has prayed constantly for me, to my father who is my favorite fan, to Ethel, a real coach's wife, and to all those in my family who are always in my corner, win or lose.

John B. McLendon, Jr.

INTRODUCTION

Basketball is an interesting, exciting game to the player, coach, and spectator when the action involves a rapid interchange of the ball from player to player and from team to team. Though it is more strenuous to the player, it is more interesting to the fan when the offense and defense are played from end-line to end-line. Various defenses employed for strategic reasons are often applied from goal to goal, but the Fast Break Offense is the only offense designed to operate on a full-court basis. All other offenses are played on a half-court area. The addition of a full-court offense as a primary or auxiliary offense will, because of its being unique in that respect, definitely enhance a coach's arsenal of winning weapons.

There are some few who speak derisively of the fast break, but there are none who refuse to use its techniques if and when circumstances are presented for the quick easy lay-up shot on the end of a long pass or two. Contrary to its reputation, the fast break is not an "aimless," "helter-skelter," "run and shoot," "fire horse" game except in the appearance of its rapid, often demoralizing, action. It is a planned attack with multiple applications; it is a designed offense which can be utilized in one or more of its several phases each time a team gains possession of the ball. It has been an often-used offense for many years, and many have enjoyed its rewards. In this text it will be analyzed, examined, and explained for purposes of adoption and application.

My experience includes having coached championship teams in high school, college, National Industrial Basketball League, A. A. U. National Tournament, international and professional basketball. Into each area I have taken the principles, philosophy, skills, and techniques pertinent to the Fast Break Offense. The break away from the stereotyped game of "set offense first and fast break when you can" to "fast break first and set offense when you have to" has added a new dimension to the game which multiplies the coach's repertoire of scoring possibilities and, equally important, allows the use of limited-ability personnel in important team-play position, a great morale factor.

The Fast Break as a primary offense is the recommended game for coaches searching for increased stature in their profession and added victories for their record.

Contents

Fast Break Basketball

fundamentals

and

fine points

Part I

FAST BREAK ORIENTATION

1

Fifteen Reasons
the Fast Break
Is a Winner

Good fortune made it possible for me to have attended school in Kansas, a state which was and is known for excellent basketball, early one-hand shooting, rugged board-work, and a general dedication to the game in which players accept very strenuous training programs as routine. My initial try-out in basketball ended in my becoming the student manager. On the bench with my first coach A. T. Edwards of Sumner High School I was introduced to an emphasis on superior conditioning combined with lightning thrusts at the opponents' goal from the old center-jump. My Junior College Coach (Sumner Branch of Kansas City Junior College) Beltron Orme, a part-time psychology teacher, found a place for me, a small player on that team, by assigning me to outrace the defense and score on the close shot afforded me by a long-pass assist from my slower but strong rebounding teammates. Naturally, I became an early devotee of a system which utilized my meager talents, speed, and stamina and helped them contribute to outstanding team success. I would not have made it by any other system.

Following, I have outlined the 15 reasons why I think the

fast break is a kind of game that can put any team with even mediocre ability into the scoring column—consistently. It has proved itself for my teams and it should for yours too. Here's why:

1. It Uses an Individual's Special Skills

I first knew the Fast Break as a winner because it could use the few special abilities of an individual. It seemed more practical from the coaching standpoint than a system that depends on all-around ability in all players.

So often, especially in the early practice season, players may fail to attract attention because their one or two special abilities may be overshadowed by other players who can execute several skills, if not exceptionally, at least reasonably well. Wherever there is a lack of players with multiple skills, individuals who can execute one skill very well may be molded together for the fast break offense. At various times and on various teams, I have had one or more players who could excel at only one of the following skills, yet when all the skills were merged and coordinated, the team functioned successfully.

1. Rebounding the defensive board.
2. Breaking repeatedly and tirelessly for the close shot.
3. Throwing the quick outlet pass.
4. Throwing the long pass accurately and quickly.
5. Getting the ball out, off the defensive boards without being tied up.
6. Getting away from and out in front of the defensive opponent.
7. Driving and/or passing off from high speed movement.
8. Dribbling well and giving the assist-type pass.
9. Shooting the open shot from the trailer positions.
10. Driving the middle lane after being in position at all times for the outlet pass.

Let me say, however, that having a squad of good players with above-average ability in all phases of the game is the more desirable situation. In many or most high schools and colleges, however, the coach will usually find himself with a limited number of all-around ability players and a larger number of players who can do only one or two things well. The fast break offense can be more effective with less all-around talent per player than any other offense. I have to go along with a system in which the coach who has relatively poor material can still think of success.

It is true that emphasizing the fast break as a *primary* offense implies a secondary offense in reserve. All teams should be prepared with more than one offense; the fast-breaking team is no exception. When the fast break is inadvisable, a companion system must be available for immediate use. If it is one which can take advantage of the strongest points in the personnel of the fast break offense, so much the better. My teams employ the Tandem-Pivot-Post offense, which gives the special abilities of my fast break players a place in the secondary scheme.

This system as I employ it utilizes two rebounders as high and low center-post men, the third rebounder as a forward, and two guards in a normal set offense position. This offers a variety of offensive scoring maneuvers for any player in the offense with scoring potential. I am offering this information only to indicate that if your fast break offense is based on the player with limited skills, your set offense (to be used when the fast break is over or is impractical) must also be a system which takes into account personnel of that kind.

2. It Helps When Your Defense Is Weak

Returning to the subject, I find that the fast break is a winner when one is forced to use players insufficiently trained in defensive fundamentals or those who fail to learn defense quickly enough to offset the offensive maneuvers of the opponents. Far be it from me to advocate the abandonment of defense, but I do know that in lieu of a defense there is still a way to win—outscore the opponents. Offense becomes a defense, a defense against loss. The undermanned defensive personnel may compensate for their glaring inability by resorting to an all-out scoring effort, allowing the regular defensive plan to become secondary in importance. You can defeat some teams if you possess only a semblance of a defense by overwhelming them with field goals.

Amplifying the foregoing statement, one may notice the number of zone defenses employed; some are used solely because of the lack of time needed to develop the good, individual, man-to-man defense. Zones are thus employed as an *offense* rather than as a *defense* since the emphasis is on the defensive rebounding and the fast break from an automatic fast break formation. On other occasions, team tactics of the man-to-man type are used with the free knowledge of individual weaknesses involved, yet with an emphasis on the immediate offensive thrust to compensate for the defensive weakness. Sometimes a press is used in this manner. On still other occasions, a coach will use a gambling, unorthodox surprise defense, knowing in his heart it is not sound but holding on to the possibility of fast breaking from it to offset the lack of sound defensive ability in his line-up. These are several examples of a plus offense overbalancing a minus defense—not a good thing to plan for, but a good thing to fall back on when other plans fail. Many good seasons have been put together by teams which have displayed offensive power and limited defensive strength.

3. It Undermines the Opponent's Stamina

Although the defense may not allow you to score as easily or as frequently as you wish, that same defense cannot stop a team from fast breaking whenever it wishes to go in a hurry. I am thinking now of the fast break not only as a scoring device but as a weapon for undermining the physical condition of the opponents.

As an example, on August 6, 1960, in Canton, Ohio, a team of mine, the Cleveland Pipers (AAU Champions in 1961), after two weeks of rigorous training, defeated the U. S. Olympic team. The team used the fast break as a scoring weapon and as a planned means of breaking down "the greatest amateur team ever assembled" to a point of physical inability to cope with our style of play. The Olympic Team, en route to Rome, listed at guard positions, Oscar Robertson, Jerry West, Les Lane, Allan Kelly, and Adrian Smith; at forward, Terry Dischinger, Bob Boozer, and Jerry Lucas; at center, Walt Bellamy, Birdie Halderson, and Darrell Imhoff. The Pipers used effectively the one chance they had. They put the fast break into high gear, adding my own strategic maneuver, the "four second rule." This rule requires every member of the team to clear the back court and be on the way to the goal or alternately to his position in the set offense in four seconds every time we get possession of the ball. Possession of the ball referred to secured rebounds, free throws made, field goals made, out of bounds, violations, and so forth. We used the fast break from the back court to a scoring position or to our set offensive positions every time we got the ball. The continued pace was too much for the Olympians and they succumbed 103–96.

Here, then, is a significant example of a team using the Fast Break to equalize or to overcome a superior foe by applying the system to wear the opponents down.

We used these and similar tactics after that August night to win 47 of 58 games in the National Industrial Basketball League and the AAU National Tournament. When I coached the touring U. S. All-Star team in its eight game sweep of the U.S.A.–U.S.S.R. series in 1961 (including four games with the Russians National, or Olympic, one and two teams), we used the fast break game as a means of survival. Our boys had to call on all their stamina and dogged determination to batter down the Soviets in an international battle of fast-breaking teams. Five of my Cleveland Pipers, John Barnhill, Tennessee State; Roger Taylor, Illinois University; Jack Adams, Eastern Kentucky State; Dan Swartz, Morehead State; and Ben Warley, Tennessee State, teamed with Gary Thompson, Iowa State and Phillip 66; Jerry Shipp, Southeast Oklahoma State and Phillip 66; Paul Newman, Stanford and New York Tapers; Jim Francis, Dartmouth and Akron Goodyears; Johnnie Cox, University of Kentucky and Akron Goodyears; Mike Moran, Marquette University and Denver Truckers; and Jerry Lucas of Ohio State to add new speed records to the international game.

4. It Provides the Best Counter to Another Fast-Breaking Team

Where the opponent forces you to play his fast-breaking game, the fast break is the best counter. In the U.S.S.R. our team found the fast break to be our saving possession. The circumstances called for our overcoming a skilled and strongly-conditioned aggregation—a difficult combination to defeat. The challenge to the player is a resounding one; in such a situation physical readiness becomes as important as skill. When you cannot stop a team from scoring, you may allow your defense to become secondary or of slight consideration. The answer may be in simply going all out offensively, abandoning all but a semblance of defense, and playing a wide-open game in an effort to outscore the opponents. Strongly-conditioned, determined players operating under such strategy may still give you a chance to get into the victory column.

The need for disciplining condition is not as apparent in other offenses often classed as half-court offenses. A player who will condition himself for the full-court game will generally eliminate those habits and practices which contribute a physical status less than the best. A lack of allegiance to training rules is quite clear and observable wherever the fast break is the game.

5. It Necessitates Conditioning

The fast break, then, is a winner because it creates the need for excellent conditioning, which in turn requires the elimination of harmful practices in the athlete's living habits. Late hours, tobacco in any form, or alcohol cannot be a part of any player's habits, and, most certainly, not if his basketball plans include the fast break offense.

The latest American Medical Association findings show that there is no longer any doubt that athletes should not smoke. Further, scientific study shows that ten inhalations of cigarette smoke may reduce the ability of the lungs to take in and utilize oxygen by as much as 50 per cent. In any close finish between well-matched athletes, the non-smoker has the edge.

Of course, there is absolutely no justification for an athlete using an alcoholic beverage at any time in his entire career.

6. It Uncovers the Weak Links

The fast break serves the coach as an "athletic X-ray" through which the true picture of the conditioning and training program is revealed. This valuable and informative service helps make winners. As far as the player is concerned, the coach gives serious attention to preparations for competition. He knows the slacker, the corner-cutter, the undisciplined, and the player who cheats on his teammates. The only way to escape detection is to "refrain and train."

"Resting on offense" is a well known way to regain or conserve physical strength during the game. "Slowing the ball down" by going through the pattern several times at medium speed in order to get organized or get a breath is out of the question in the fast break game. The fast break offense and the complementing pressing defense leave "no rest for the weary."

7. It Inspires Teamwork

The full-court offense is a winner when one considers how it involves the assignment of certain definite and equally important responsibilities to each player and, in so doing, inspires the highest kind of teamwork. If one phase of the offense is not carried through, it will become ineffective, and some secondary idea of offense will have to be employed. Many of the half-court offenses rely on individual prowess for the scoring action, using only one or two players and only occasionally more than three. The fast break system makes teamwork a five-player concept. Teamwork is a morale-building factor. Realizing the importance of each segment of the whole as an important part of the successful endeavor encourages team members to shift their interest from individual to team statistics. Team rebounding, team field goal percentages, team loss-of-ball figures are items which gain in importance as the concept of true team play is realized. Minimizing the individual performance in favor of a team operation is very often a refreshing shift in emphasis and is appreciated thoroughly by the players.

In 1946 I coached the North Carolina College "Eagles" (Central Intercollegiate Athletic Association) with their never-to-be-forgotten four "mighty mites" (four players 5 feet 4 inches to 5 feet 7 inches, three of whom were starters) to its first tournament championship (the final game ended in a triple overtime). The greatest testimonial to the teamwork and outstanding ability of this team was the failure of the sportswriters to place a single player on their all-conference team. It was not only the startling speed, dexterity, and endless stamina which marked the undersized players, but their thoroughly team-oriented approach to the game which made them so remarkably successful. The players were no better in their technique. Individuality, however, was secondary to teamwork. I repeat that the nature of the fast break system which they played inspired, in fact required, the team play they so completely exemplified. Each player in the fast break offense is as important as and depends as much on the other players for the success of the total plan. The attitudes the fast break generates are the attitudes desired by coaches.

8. It is Best for Consistent Performance

The attack centers around the optimum scoring area (within 15 feet of the goal) and the optimum scoring shot, the driving lay-up which results in a score or a defensive foul. The "cold night" occurs less frequently and the "cold shooting game" ceases to be the coach's nightmare, because the major scoring effort is concentrated at the end of the fast break close to the basket.

9. It Makes the Game Exciting to Play and Watch

The fast-breaking game is an exciting game for the players, coach, and spectators. It is a winner at the turnstiles (in some circles a point to consider), but, more importantly, it is a game of increased challenge to the young contestant. The challenge lies in the player's learning to make the most of the many choices confronting him. The high-speed game requires quick sound reactions, lightning-quick decisions, and corresponding physical and mechanical adjustments to meet the ever-changing situations. The application of speed in utilizing the full-court area increases the probability of error, the circumstances of error and recovery, and the need to adjust to a rapidly-forming defensive counteraction. The question of endurance becomes more important. All of these factors make this kind of game interesting, entertaining, and educational to the participant and onlookers alike.

10. High Speed Play Produces Versatile Players

Speed is an essential ingredient for better player performance. Learning to execute fundamental skills properly at a faster pace is the player's problem and the coach's task. When mastered, it has its full reward. Increasing the speed of the pass, pivot, turn, change of direction, dribble, and shooting develops the player from ordinary to outstanding. Players who can skillfully execute basketball techniques at high speed will show up as more skillful performers under slower speed conditions. The reverse is not true. Consequently, when an opposing team slows down a fast-breaking team, the advantage is still with the fast team. The slow team, however, when rushed through their paces at a faster speed than they are accustomed to, will usually become demoralized from multiplying floor mistakes, not to mention exhaustion. The fast-breaking team acquires those techniques which mark it as the more versatile. The skills and techniques employable in the fast break offense are usable in practically all other offenses, but the opposite is not often true. This conclusion indicates that the fast break is the primary offense one should learn and teach.

Despite the need for the addition of extra speed, there is usually a corresponding added interest and extra industry applied to the system by the player. The offense itself is simple and is easy to teach and learn as far as position and duties are concerned. In fact, it is the simplest offense in terms of mechanics. Therefore, it is a good offense for average players and a great offense for expert players, inasmuch as players in a simplified system can spend added time on self-improvement.

11. It Complements Various Defenses

The fast break is an offense which complements certain defenses to such an extent that the defense may be regarded as part of the offense. The application of various zone defenses, pressing defenses, and man-to-man and zone defensive tactics which give the offense the ball with a rapidly developing scoring potential can actually "trigger" the fast break. Few offenses possess this unusual and powerful advantage. (A full discussion of this point is in Chapter V.)

12. It Has a Successful Background

The fast break has been successful for years. It is time-tested and has met the test of competition well. This may sound like too simple a statement, but the test of success is a valid one. Many teams come to mind, various national collegiate champions and many scholastic champions, which have used this offense, but the most prolific winner utilizing the fast break is the N.B.A. Boston Celtics team. Despite the fact that their personnel leaves little to be desired, the system to which they are dedicated carries them a greater part of the way to victory. I think that a shift to any other system would put them in the contender's class. Three consecutive N.A.I.A. championships, one National Industrial League championship, and one National A.A.U. championship are some of my own testimonials to the success of the fast break offense.

13. Team Organization Is Simplified by the Fast Break

The responsibilities of each player are clearly understood, and, as has been mentioned, exceptional skill is not as necessary to success in this method of play. In fact, the organization of the team for success is centered around the question, "Who will carry out the fast break idea?" and not necessarily, "Who is capable?"

Organization, then, is based mainly on the selection of players with some degree of ability, of course, but also with a large degree of determination, acquired physical stamina, and desire to excel. It is not as difficult to find the player with *skill* as it is to find the player with *will*.

Basketball and other sports serve youth best when there is a large and obvious place in the sport for the intrinsic values of the game. There are more of these values in basketball played with the fast break offense than in any other, simply because of the physical and psychological involvement of the player.

14. It Demoralizes the Defense

The high pressure tactics of the fast break are calculated to disorganize and, subsequently, demoralize the defense. The fast break exploits one of the basic stratagems of the game of basketball, which is to force the opponent to deviate from the game they have planned to play. This idea refers to the defensive game as well as the offensive game.

The team defending against a fast-breaking team is similar to a right-handed boxer meeting a "southpaw." The right-hander is facing an unusual opponent. The "southpaw" is facing a usual opponent. The right-hander has the greater and more special adjustment to make, not only defensively but offensively too.

The fast break opponent forces a team to reorganize its defensive plan. Very often this reorganization is of an emergency nature and may not have a strong relationship to the previously and regularly used defense. Unless, however, the defense is well-planned and practiced and is one which can meet the multiplicity of attack options, chaos is the likely result.

Furthermore, in order to protect themselves more successfully, the team opposing the running team must alter its *offense* to insure proper placement or location of personnel for exact defensive responsibility. When this fact is not considered, it is possible for a team to fail in its offensive functions.

When adequate preparation has not been made and an opponent with only a normal defense meets a fast-breaking club, chances are the offense will completely demoralize the defensive team before the evening is over.

15. It's Modern Basketball

Finally, the fast break is a winner because it is the game the world is playing. All the countries of the world play by International Rules except the U.S.A. The 30-second rule, which requires a team to make a field goal attempt within 30 seconds after it gains possession of the ball, speeds up the game and removes the stall tactics from play. It does not remove the control phase of the game. Contrary to general opinion, the fast break can be exercised with as much control as there is in many other offenses.

International Rules, then, don't allow anything less than a

fast moving offense, and there must usually be a preliminary offensive move to the set offensive position approximating, or similar to, the fast break game. The control factor in the game is limited to a timed, constructive, offensive idea designed to result in scoring, as opposed to the control idea, which allows ball withholding to become the primary objective.

These rules govern Olympic Basketball competition where the most coveted of team game prizes, the gold medal in basketball, must be contended for every four years. Therefore, the American player should continually have access to the kind of game which, in its main theme, approximates the international game. This will keep him in some degree of readiness for the increasingly difficult task of overcoming world opponents. Various rules such as the 19-foot lane (at the base line), the aforementioned 30-second rule, the absence of a 10-second line, the 2-only, noncumulative time-outs per half, the 2-shot free throw during the last 5 minutes, the take-the-ball-out-of-bounds rule for every foul except the one committed when the player is in the act of shooting, the non-allowance of the "3-point" play, the time-out called by the coach only (and when the timer gets the attention of the referee), are all rules sufficiently alien to our U.S. game to place us at a disadvantage.

Those teams using the fast break seldom find a possible 30-second limit a factor in their game. This game is the game upon which the U.S. must rely for maintaining a respectable position in world basketball. We will fall short of our ambition any day we fail to include this offense in our preparation for international competition. For this reason alone, the full-court game is a winning game, one to be utilized in all areas of competition, Olympic basketball not excluded.

To summarize:

Fifteen Reasons Why the Fast Break Is a Winner

1. It can successfully employ players who have limited all-around talent but who have one or two special abilities.

2. It offsets the lack of sufficiently trained defensive personnel.

3. It can break an opposing team physically and decrease their advantage of skill and size.

4. It is the best answer to opponents who force your team to run.

5. It creates the need for excellent conditioning and health practices which insure this status.

6. It serves as a detector of physical unreadiness and physical limitation.

7. It inspires teamwork basketball.

8. It is the best game for consistent performance since it utilizes the close shooting attack in the "optimum scoring area."

9. It is an exciting, entertaining game to the player, coach, and spectator. It has great appeal to the participant and fan.

10. It is the most versatile offense.

11. It complements more defenses than any other offense.

12. It has been used most successfully by many teams in all areas of competition. It is a winner by record.

13. It allows for ease of team organization.

14. It is a high-pressure offense designed to disorganize opposing team defense and limit opposing team offense.

15. It is basic to continued preparedness for International competition.

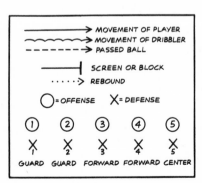

Key to Illustrations

The key at the left is to be used to interpret the illustrations which follow throughout the book.

2

Fast Break Principles

and Philosophy

In basketball the fast break is a widely known and widely used means of advancing the ball toward the offensive goal with greater than average speed, usually in two or more lanes of attack, with the intention of outnumbering and thus overwhelming the defensive players in the *optimum scoring area* (Diagram 2) who may have retreated or who may be in the process of retreating to defend that zone. Primary objectives, then, are to gain the numerical advantage in the optimum scoring area, to outmaneuver the defense, and to score before the defense can recover to an organized position.

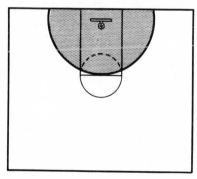

Diagram 2

When employing the fast break as a primary offense, a team utilizes swift movement down court *each* time it gains possession of the ball. Such a team hopes to display the necessary passing dexterity while in accelerated motion, shooting accuracy in the drive-in shot, high-percentage shooting in the 15-foot area, and a dependency on excellent physical conditioning in continued attempts to execute the offensive plan.

The Opportunity Break

One philosophy involving the employment of the fast break has the team going only when an opportunity presents itself. Usually, in this situation the offensive team, through errors in ball-handling and passing, presents the opportunity to the defense. Often, this results in one of the defense's lone players (now on offense) breaking into the clear toward his goal with a driving dribble or in his receiving a pass from his teammate who has capitalized on a similar mistake. In this "opportunity break" the players move quickly to the position of numerical advantage, which, as previously defined, means any one of the following:

a. One offensive player with no defensive player between himself and the goal.
b. Two offensive players versus one on defense (Diagram 3).
c. Three offensive players versus one on defense (Diagram 4).

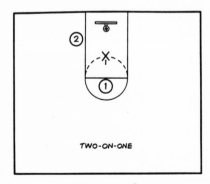

TWO-ON-ONE

Diagram 3

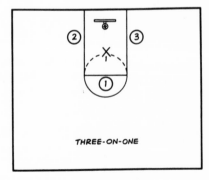

THREE-ON-ONE

Diagram 4

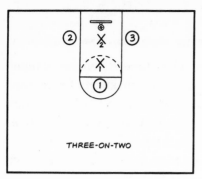

THREE-ON-TWO

Diagram 5

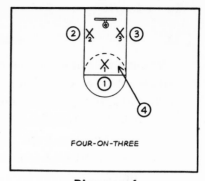

FOUR-ON-THREE

Diagram 6

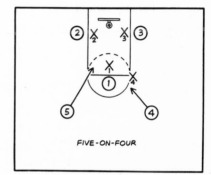

FIVE-ON-THREE

Diagram 7

FIVE-ON-FOUR

Diagram 8

d. Three offensive players versus two defensive players (Diagram 5).

e. Four offensive players versus three defensive players (Diagram 6).

f. Five offensive players versus three defensive players (Diagram 7).

g. Five offensive players versus four defensive players (Diagram 8).

The philosophy of the "opportunity break" might be stated by a coach to his team in this way: "Wait until you get an opportunity to use your fast break; take advantage of any loose balls, poorly executed passes, fumbles, or other errors. Under these conditions, get the ball and go! Otherwise, hold up."

The "opportunity break" holds a big place in basketball. It is a secondary offense, however, inasmuch as it is employed only in answer to certain types of opposing offenses or as a stratagem in phases of some games where defensive forcing would not be wise. Such a game calls for quickness of response, ability to anticipate, and practically all of the offensive abilities needed in the continuous, forcing fast break, except that it is not a full-court game and lacks even limited pressure aspects. However, almost all teams will employ the fast break from an opportunity.

The Forcing Break

The philosophy of the fast break to which I subscribe includes the "opportunity break" but goes the big step beyond the waiting game to the "forcing" fast break. I mean by this term "forcing" that the defensive game of the breaking team must be so interwoven with the offense that it appears to be, and actually becomes, a part of the offense. The defense forces a multiplication of the number of times the offense is to gain possession of the ball. Waiting for mistakes to give the ball to your team or for the opponents to shoot so you can possibly grab the defensive rebound is not enough. The "forcing" fast break goes after the ball! This game forces situations which launch the attack, creates conditions which make the fast break the logical maneuver. Its complementing defenses disarrange the half-court offenses and capitalize on the forced deviation from preplanned attack to thrust continuously into scoring territory.

The Pressing Defenses

Needless to say, there are many team defenses and many defensive maneuvers employed which force the offense into "turnovers." The best advertised recently is the successful full-court, zone-press defense employed by two-time NCAA University Champion UCLA (1964 and 1965). Significantly enough, the NCAA College Division Champion of 1965, Evansville College, the National Association of Intercollegiate Athletics 1965 Champion, Central State College of Ohio, and the National

AAU Champions, the Armed Forces Team, all used pressing ("forcing") tactics as their principal defensive-offensive weapon. These teams, though playing against good, ball-handling teams, many of which were intent on a ball control game, successfully "kept the pressure on" throughout the game, thus "multiplying" their own offensive opportunities. "Pressure" is kept on teams by planned techniques. The following represent a few of those which may be taught:

Back Court

1. A strong defender versus the opposing playmaker.
2. A strong double-team on the most eligible receiver on the throw-in after a field goal made.
3. Strongest pressure on the third man to become involved in bringing the ball out of the back court.
4. Forcing the ball to the sidelines (or center, depending on the defensive idea being developed) for the "sideline trap."
5. Forcing the player to the "corners" for a single-man attack or double-team ("corner trap"). The "corners" I refer to are the four in the back court and the four in the front court. The front-court corners at the ten-second line are the best "traps" for the defense.
6. Interceptions of the pass forced upward (the loft pass) and the slow, long pass.
7. Forcing the opponent into faster speeds than those to which he has been accustomed.
8. Varying the defensive tactics.

Front Court

1. Attacking the ball at all times and compensating for the change of ball position.
2. Overplaying the possible receiver.
3. Double-teaming close offensive play.
4. Double-teaming a single player isolated from his teammates.

5. Pressuring the pivot man with zone tactics in front play, double-teaming on and off.
6. Overplaying the offensive player who has the ball to force him to an area where he may be attacked with team tactics.
7. Using a team rebounding plan for the defensive rebounds.
8. Attacking the player who has used up his dribble and his nearest receiver.
9. Continuous arm, hand position harassment.
10. Employing changing team defenses.

If you wish to capitalize with big returns on the results of the foregoing defensive measures, the fast break is the logical answer.

Lanes

To accomplish best results with the numerical overload (two-on-one, three-on-two, etc.) the players move speedily into two to five lanes (Diagram 9) which are described as follows:

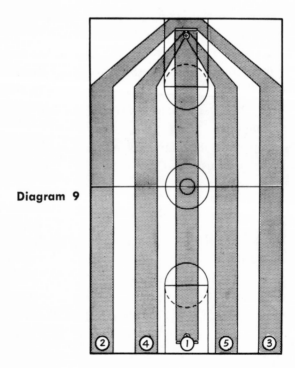

Diagram 9

Lane 1—The middle six to eight feet of the court from goal to goal.

Lane 2—The left side of the court from the side line to six feet in bounds and extending from the end line to a point opposite the top of the circle at the opposite end of the court and from that point angling to the goal.

Lane 3—Same as Lane 2 except that it is on the right side of the court.

Lane 4—Extends from end line to end line, from outside the center lane to the left and is about six feet in width.

Lane 5—Extends from end line to end line, from outside the center lane to the right and is about six feet in width.

The purpose of numbering is for identification of the lane only.

From various conditions forced on the opponents by the defensive tactics being used, the fast break forms after possession of the ball into first a three-lane attack (Lanes 1, 2, 3 in Diagram 9), followed quickly by two trailing players in Lanes 4 and 5. Occasionally, it happens in the "opportunity break" mentioned earlier that an individual fast break is managed by a player breaking with an intercepted pass or breaking away from the defense to receive a pass from his teammate. More often, however, there are two players versus one defensive player. Most often, there are three versus two players. In fact, the three-on-two situation seems to occur more frequently than any other situation involving an offensive overload. On all occasions, ball handling, passing, dribbling, and scoring must take place before the defense matches the offense and organizes to prevent the goal.

The Three-Lane Attack

The essence of fast break success, as I see it, is to get the two players on one or the three-on-two into scoring position. My statistics and observations over the years show that the best combination for fast break scoring is the three-lane attack, since practically all teams are prepared to have two men back on defense as a matter of offensive balance, if not for fast break defense. The *third man* in the *third lane* is the *key* man. He must fill the third lane across the mid-court *before* the third defensive player can retreat across the mid-line to present an organized defensive effort by three men. Getting the vital, third player back on defense is the big problem imposed on a defensive team by an offensive team using the three-lane fast break.

The fast break is the only offense which seeks to operate by immediately placing more offensive players than defensive players nearest the goal. In other offenses the offense begins with the entire defense between the ball and the goal, after which, there is an attempt to displace one or more defensive players so that the offense may gain the advantage. I like the fast break as a primary offense. If that offense and its many variations and follow-ups should fail, I will then use a half-court system as a secondary offense, thus giving me a "double-barreled" attack at the enemy. It is my intention, however, to use all of our fast break resources in an effort to avoid using the secondary offense. We will "break every time and set up only when we have to."

Coaching Hints

In support of the philosophy of the game as I have stated it, here are a few coaching hints which are important for your consideration and possible adoption:

1. Condition your team for the fast break game. Your players will then be physically ready to play any other game, for any other game requires less stamina.
2. Think "fast break, attack" at all times. The player's first look is down court. Get the fast break started, "fill the lanes!"
3. Consider defense as a part of offense, not merely a means to stop the opponents from scoring. Force the opponents to give up the ball.

4. Force the opponents to play your game.
5. Keep the opponents under pressure throughout the game. Do not let up! Give them no rest!
6. Encourage each player to do his part, that part of the game for which he is especially adapted. The fast break allows for specialization. *Specialize* until the player learns more skills, then add a little more to his job.
7. Plan every phase of practice to carry over to some aspect of the game. Practice periods should contain a majority of fast break skills and techniques. Do not practice unrelated skills.
8. Return frequently, almost daily, to fundamentals: passing, dribbling, pivoting, sprinting, lay-up, and close shooting.
9. Add speed to the fundamentals *after* they have been mastered.
10. Sell the game to your players. They must believe in any offense you use, but a greater selling job must be done with the fast break because of its greater demands.
11. Convince your players that they must be uniquely prepared for the special demands of the game. Make them believe they are special. They are!
12. Keep the game mechanically simple. It is the simplest offense to understand, but it requires the most "heart" to make it go.

Summary

Here are the principals of the fast break summarized:

1. Get the ball by concentration on defensive rebounding.
2. Release it to the key dribbler in the attack.
3. Get two players down court ahead of the ball and behind the defense in the offensive lanes.
4. Maneuver the ball to the middle of the court to the offensive circle area.
5. Shoot the high-percentage shot in the optimum scoring area.
6. Follow-up the offensive rebound.

7. Utilize the fast break trailer offense.
8. Take advantage of the free-lance opportunities.
9. Make use of other points of fast break inception other than the defensive rebound and apply the same principles.
10. Get the ball through strong defensive play.
11. Go, run, drive, on each occasion of possession.
12. Give each man his responsibility in keeping with his special ability.

Part II

DEVELOPING THE FAST BREAK OFFENSE

3

The Primary Inception Point
of the Fast Break

The fast break offense is a full-court game beginning from any place on the court. There are several points from which the offense is initiated with more frequency than others.

These inception points are:

1. The defensive rebound after a field goal attempt is missed.
2. The end line throw-in after a successful field goal.
3. The defensive rebound after a missed free throw.
4. The end line throw-in after a successful free throw.
5. Held ball situations from the center circle or back-court circle.
6. Miscellaneous origins:
   a. Pass interceptions
   b. Recovery of loose balls
   c. Stealing the ball

Get the Rebound

The *primary* inception point is the defensive rebound which originates from the missed field goal attempt. There are usually one or more defensive rebounds available for each field goal made. The number of defensive rebounds may be substantially decreased by teams trained in offensive rebounding

29

techniques. Nevertheless, the defensive rebound is the defense's main weapon in gaining possession of the ball and in beginning the fast break.

Fast break possibilities vary from one defensive area to another, depending on the type of defense employable in each area. The area nearest the opponent's basket, of course, is the place where all rebounding takes place and where the fast break most often starts. The defensive possibilities of different areas of the court are discussed in Part IV.

In terms of its ability to launch the fast break quickly, the zone defense should be termed "zone offense." In an offensive capacity the zone defense has much more value as a team technique than is found in its defensive claims.

The 2-1-2

The 2-1-2 zone offers the best possible formation for fast break purposes. The 2-1-2 alignment of personnel is also the best formation to use when teaching fast break responsibilities (Diagram 10). From the placement of the 2-1-2 defensive team, the general plan of attack when the defensive rebound is secured by players X3 and X5 is to pass the ball out to 02,

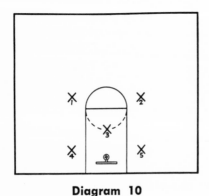

Diagram 10

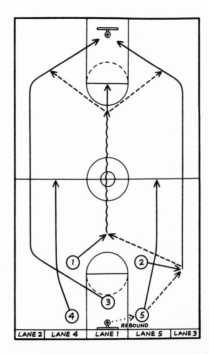

Diagram 11

who waits for the outlet pass opposite the foul line along the offensive, right side line. If X4 rebounds, X1 becomes the outlet pass receiver on the offensive, left side line. From this point, there are many variations in advancing the ball and in filling lanes 1 to 5 (Diagram 11). X1 and X2 are in the best position for receiving the outlet pass or for moving down court. X3, X4, X5 are in the best position for the 3-man defensive rebound triangle.

The simplest 2-1-2 fast break plan works as follows (Diagram 9. Defense is now changed to offense with appropriate symbols):

If the ball is rebounded by 05, he passes out to 02. 01 cuts to the center lane (1) to receive the pass from 02 and dribbles down center lane (1) as player 02 takes right side-line lane (3).

03 or 04, whoever can get there first, takes lane 2. One of the two, 03 or 04, who did not break and 05 become the trailing players ("trailers") in lanes 4 and 5.

If the ball is rebounded by 03, the same plan is followed except 04 or 05 takes lane 2 (Diagram 12). The remaining two players trail in lanes 4 and 5.

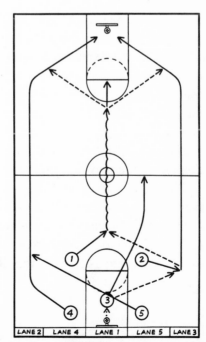

Diagram 12

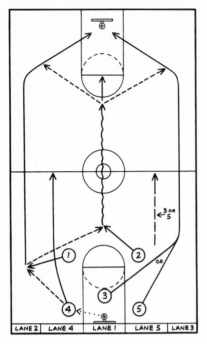

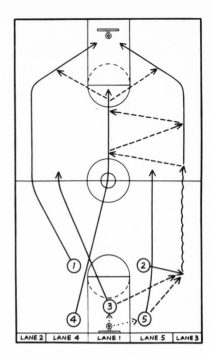

| LANE 2 | LANE 4 | LANE 1 | LANE 5 | LANE 3 |

Diagram 13

| LANE 2 | LANE 4 | LANE 1 | LANE 5 | LANE 3 |

Diagram 14

If the ball is rebounded by 04 (Diagram 13), 01 takes the outlet pass and lane 2. 02 receives the ball from 01 and takes lane 1 with the driving dribble. 03 or 05 takes lane 3. The remaining two players trail in lanes 4 and 5.

In the foregoing plan and the variations based solely on which player rebounds, the players going to the outside lanes must speedily move out in front of the ball and behind the defense as they fill their lanes, in order to depress the defensive, back-court men. This simple maneuver allows the dribbling center-lane player to advance the ball. If the defense does not retreat, the ball goes to the cutter in the lane offering least difficulty for the driving lay-up—guard's choice.

The outside lanes and the players who will fill them "out in front of the ball" are the keys to successful attack.

Probably the fastest three-lane fast break possible depends on the ability of a forward or center to "handle the middle lane" (Diagram 14). In a situation where 03 or 05 gets the re-

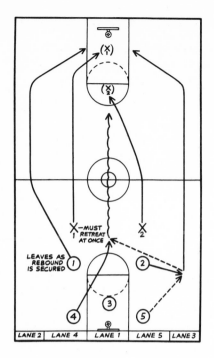

Diagram 15

LANE 2 | LANE 4 | LANE 1 | LANE 5 | LANE 3

bound, the same rebound pass out plan is followed: as the out-let pass goes to 02, for example, 02 passes the ball to 04, a forward, who takes the center lane opposite the dribbler, or 02 dribbles fast down lane 3. Directly as the ball is passed to 04, lane 2 is filled by 01 moving very fast down court ahead of teammate 04. This quick 3-on-2 move has two or three quick option passes, depending on defensive reaction, for a fast two points. 03 and 05 are the trailers in lanes 4 and 5.

When 04 takes the center lane and 01 breaks fast and wide to lane 2, one defensive player, X1, must go with 01, or the ball will be passed to this free-cutting guard (Diagram 15). If the defender X1 retreats as he should, 04 and 02 are 2-on-1 versus the remaining defender, X2. X2 must play two men, 04 in lane 1 and 02 in lane 3. He must have help (and fast) or the 3-on-2 overload will develop in the optimum scoring area for a decided offensive advantage.

There are other offensive variations possible from the 2-1-2

33

zone, however, the foregoing fast break patterns are those which are simplest to operate from the defensive rebound and are at the same time those most likely to succeed.

Other Zone Defenses

The 2-1-2 zone is not the only zone defense quickly adaptable and changeable for fast break purposes. The 2-3 zone is similar in alignment, and, although the defensive assignments for each player are different from those in the 2-1-2, the offensive assignments from the defensive rebound situation are the same (Diagram 16). A team may convert from the 2-3 zone (or any other zone, for that matter) to the 2-1-2 as the field goal attempt is made. Diagram 17 shows how the 3-2 zone defense converts to a 2-1-2 for maximum fast break potential. Diagram 18, showing the 1-3-1 zone and its fast break possibility from the defensive rebound, may be considered a slower-developing pattern than from other zones, yet, for rebounding alone, it is difficult to beat. A fast break pattern involving only one outlet pass receiver, as is the case in the 1-3-1, may have difficulty in its initial stages and may be inadequate to outspeed organized defensive coverage.

It is a fact that a zone of any alignment must convert or break down into a 2-1-2, and the same offensive responsibilities are listed for each position (as in Diagram 10) regardless of the previous defensive assignments. Another way of stating this

Diagram 16   **Diagram 17**

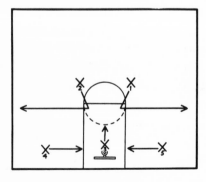

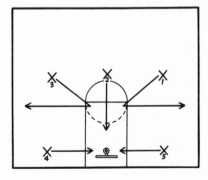

fact is, "regardless of the zone defense used, the 2-1-2 alignment is the formation you fall into for the fast break." It is the
best, original arrangement for any fast break plan. Three men
on the defensive backboard, one man to receive the outlet pass,
and an alternate receiver or lead man out in front of the ball—
these are the basic ingredients for the successful running game.
Any zone or rebound-securing technique which cannot provide
these ingredients with speed need not be incorporated into a
fast break system.

On any given night, you may find my team using any variation of one or the other of the zone defenses, but when the ball
goes up (in a field goal attempt) the old reliable three-man
zone rebound triangle is quickly formed with guards readying
themselves for outlet pass reception and down-court progress.
I submit that, regardless of whether the fast break is used or
not, the conversion of any defense to a 2-1-2 defensive pattern
for rebounding advantage is a sound maneuver for any coach's
game.

A word of caution here in regard to the rebounding potential of any zone: The potential is actually related to the
assigned mechanics of the three defensive rebounders. Their assignments must be such that during their slides (movement to
the ball and to the ball handlers) they must not be so far out
of position that it becomes impractical for them to recover for
the rebounding job.

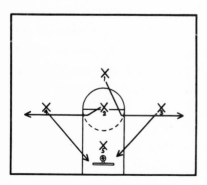

Diagram 18

4

Secondary Inception Points

1. End Line Throw-in

There are other points of origin for the fast break. The secondary point, the point from which the second most frequent number of opportunities for the fast break occur, is the *end line throw-in after a field goal has been scored* by the opponent. This point of inception, while recognized, is seldom employed. One reason for this is the extreme physical hardship involved in fulfilling the assigned tasks; another is that there is less frequency of gaining an advantage at the scoring end of the court when in this situation because the defense has its longest time to organize. Furthermore, after a field goal is scored, the team which becomes the defensive team thinks defensively and, in doing so, is psychologically less vulnerable to surprise attack. On the other hand, there is a brief moment directly after scoring when the defense relaxes. It is this moment when the quick throw-in is a most valuable part of the fast break offense. Diagram 19 illustrates a formation which provides the fast action required to give the advantage to the team with the ball. The responsibilities of each player are as follows:

The player X5, who aside from being usually assigned to defense the opposing team's pivot player and who is instructed to block-out his man 05 away from the offensive rebound and

36

secure the defensive rebound, is the logical player whose added duty it is to initiate the fast break from this point. X5 should have an inside position on 05 next to the backboard and goal. Whether he can out-rebound the offense or not, his position should be such that, as the score is made (and before the ball touches the floor, if possible), he retrieves the ball, takes it quickly out of bounds, runs two to three steps along the base line (depending on how many it takes to sight his receiver and make certain a possible interception can be by-passed), and throws the ball in to X1 or X2, whichever is quickest in getting to the side line area in the outlet-pass–receiving spot. His job is not finished. He then follows his pass with a fast movement into the lane next to the side line to which he passed the ball. He follows this lane, which is lane 3, all the way to the scoring area unless he sees three players ahead of him, in which event, he becomes a trailing player filling lane 4 or 5 (also in Diagram 19).

Many teams, especially those using forms of half-court defense, will turn their backs on the ball momentarily as they

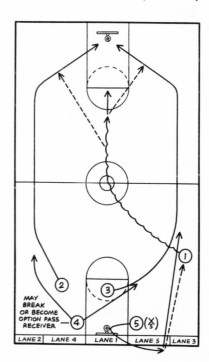

Diagram 19

retreat to their defensive positions. This momentary lapse is helpful to the effectiveness of the end line throw-in technique.

Regardless of whether individuals on the opposing team turn their backs or not, the quick throw-in produces a problem for the defense. In fact it keeps the pressure on the defense. This is one of the objectives of the offense. Nothing is more detrimental to the morale of a team than to be forced into a continuous fast break to a defensive position to halt the continuous offense. Other assignments involving player 03 and 04 are important. Since X5 (05) is the player assigned to execute the throw-in pass, each of his fellow rebounders, X3 and X4, now 03 and 04, having finished with their rebounding duties, are to get out in front of the ball, preferably filling lane 3 as indicated in Diagram 19 (but filling other lanes if the coach's plan calls for it). If there are already three players ahead of 03 and 04, either or both become the trailing players and fill-in lanes 4 and 5.

01 or 02 takes the pass-in from X5 (now 05). Either of the two which does not receive the pass immediately breaks downcourt using lane 2. The player receiving the inlet-pass drives with his dribble to lane 1 (the center lane), following it toward the scoring area, passing off in a 3-on-1 or 3-on-2 situation to the player in lane 2 or 3.

When there is a defensive player assigned to stop the inlet-pass (as there often is when this fast break idea is used), there may be a need to have 03 or 04, whichever does not break, to wait on the option pass-in on the side line opposite the pass-receiving position of 01 or 02. A maneuver limiting the effectiveness of a defensive guard assigned to 01 or 02 will be described in Chapter 9.

2. Missed Free Throw

The third point of fast break inception is the *defensive rebound after a missed free throw*. The position of players preliminary to a missed free throw is almost uniform inasmuch as the rules require two inside, defending, rebounding forwards.

The offense practically always has one player assigned to the free-throw shooter, but the location of the two guards is a big variable. Their varied position, combined with the assignments of the other three players, presents a wide differentiation in attack from this point.

Diagram 20 shows a very quick fast break from the missed free throw. The inside rebounder on the defensive right passes out to 03, who, having covered the shooter and blocked him away from the offensive rebound, takes a position on the offensive, right side line to receive the pass-out.

Players who have become well-coordinated in playing together may be instructed to work the defensive tap-out to player 03, giving added speed to the offense. 03 quickly moves to the outside position, depending on the side to which the ball rebounds, taking the ball from the defensive rebounder who taps the ball from the height of his jump.

From here, any one of previous fast break plans may be used as a follow-up, with 03 taking the ball to the center and 01 and 02 filling lanes 1 and 2. If the number three man, 03, cannot manage the necessary skills for lane 1, this plan probably

Diagram 20   **Diagram 21**

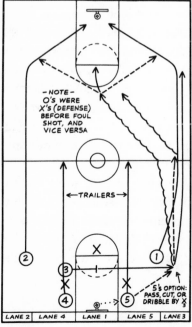
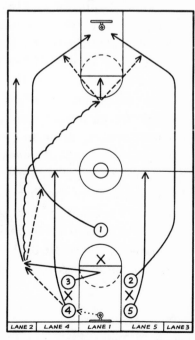

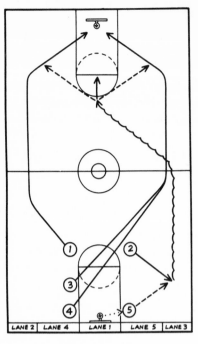

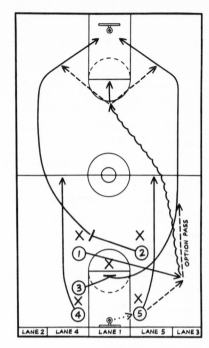

Diagram 22   **Diagram 23**

will not count in your scoring column. If rebounder number 4 gets the ball, the reverse of the preceding plan is followed (Diagram 21).

An alternate plan (Diagram 22) based on the same offensive assignments previously discussed (in relation to the fast break from the defensive rebound) is one in which 05 passes in to 02, who takes the center lane on the drive with rebounder 03 or 04 taking lane 3; 01 has long since filled lane 2. Care must be exercised by 05 on the outlet pass since during the free throw the defense is set and X1 and X2 can play 01 and 02 tightly for an interception. 01 and 02 may resort to a preliminary screening move to give 01 a clear shot at the incoming pass (Diagram 23). However, this must be timed to avoid any delay of the outlet pass getting to 01 or 02.

Diagram 24 is the first of two unusual, and to some extent unorthodox, plans to be suggested. Three possible receivers for the outlet pass from 05 break in the same direction for the outlet-passer's choice. 01 to the deep corner down court, 02 to the regular outlet pass receiving spot, 03 to the center court side

40

line (after rebounding, block-out duties). The objective is to get the pass in and down court against a disorganized defense. 03 is usually the free receiver, although the long pass may go well once or twice a game.

Diagram 25, a second unorthodox but frequently successful plan, is a variation of a formation occasionally used where both 01 and 02 are stationed deep down court. The ball is passed to 02 (or 01, depending on which side rebounds) as 02 comes up court for the half-court, outlet pass. The opposite guard remains deep, pinning his defense X1. 02 reverses with his dribble going to the center lane. 03 (or 04) fills lane 3 for the 3-on-2 offensive overload.

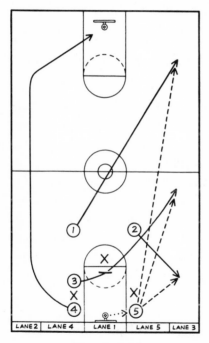

Diagram 24

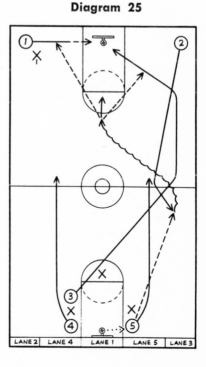

Diagram 25

Diagram 26 shows 03 in an alternate maneuver taking the outlet pass from 05. 03 passes to 02. 02 maneuvers to the center lane and passes to 01, who is in lane 2, or to 03, who has filled lane 3. 04 and 05 follow-up in lanes 4 and 5.

3. After a Free Throw is Made

The fourth point of fast break inception occurs during the time directly *after a free throw made*. The use of the fast break from this point encounters the following difficulties:

1. The defense is set. There are no players in motion; therefore, the maximum individual defense can be applied to individual offensive players.
2. Inasmuch as the fast break can be anticipated, a team defense can be put in operation.
3. Organized defense is possible to realize between the time the free throw is made and the action of taking the ball out of bounds and passing it in to a receiver.

Despite these apparently insurmountable obstacles to a possible fast break move, there is still the fact that the defense must always second guess the movements of the offense. Furthermore, the defense automatically retreats (unless a full-court press is being applied, in which case an entirely new concept of offense must be employed) and in doing so allows the advantage in this situation to return to the offense. It is also possible to establish an offensive advantage by coordinating the out-of-bounds throw-in and the pass-in reception in such a way as to give the positional advantage to the offense, if not the numerical advantage.

Diagram 27 indicates a plan for the realization of one advantage or the other. 05 has been designated prior to the game as the player who will take the ball out of the nets, out of bounds and pass it in-bounds with a fast pass to 02. 02 will have faked a down-court break and then will move in and over to the side line position opposite the top of the free-throw circle. 02 than dribbles down the side line and to the center

Diagram 26

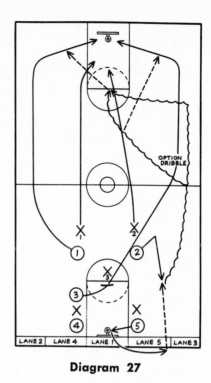

Diagram 27

if he can beat X2 or X3, whoever has remained for the task of containing 02. 03, after blocking out the free-throw shooter X3, breaks very fast to lane 3. 01, on anticipation of the successful free throw, has filled lane 2 and has sped to the base line for the pass from 02 if the defense does not retreat or to cause the defense to retreat so the center lane will be open for the advance of the center-lane dribbler 02. X3, having retreated to cover 03, is not in position to stop 02. An analysis of this fast break operation brings out the fact that the plan depends on 02 outmaneuvering his defensive man in a situation which actually isolates the two players and allows 02 such an opportunity. With the offensive players 01 and 03 out ahead of the ball almost instantly, with X4 and X5 being occupied by 04 and 05, or at least behind 02 by 25 feet, the center of the

43

court belongs to 02. Diagram 28 shows a variation of the fore-going plan which has 03 receiving the ball and, in effect, tak-ing the role of 02 as shown in Diagram 27.

4. Held or Jump Ball

Held ball or jump ball situations form a fifth fast break inception point. Reference is made to a held ball by team A which results in a jump at the circle in front of team B's goal or at the circle in the center of the court. Team A, if controlling the tip, may use any number of ways to get the fast break basket. Since it is usually clear to the offense which player will get the tip, a screen on one or more defensive players should be effected to clear at least one man to assist in bringing about the needed 2-on-1 or 3-on-2 situation.

Inasmuch as the defense is likely to be better organized in a jump ball situation than in the previous situations involving inception points, the use of the fourth and fifth man in the fast break plan is advised (see Chapter 10).

Diagrams 29, 30, and 31 show how a quick attack on the scoring area can be developed from a jump ball at the back court circle or at the center circle. In Diagram 29, where the tip can be controlled, 05 taps the ball to 04, located directly in front of the jumpers. With a quick flip or a jump pass he gives the ball to 03, who, having anticipated the control, breaks fast to outside lane 3 (so the defense will have to turn his back to the pass) and down court. 01 cuts off a screen by 02 and takes the opposite outside lane 2. After the pass, 04 moves to the free throw lane; 05 and 02 remain in the back court as safety defense men. This play is also used from the center-court circle.

Diagram 30 shows a tip going to the side to 03, who moves into the ball to take it and pass to 01, who cuts off a rear screen by 04 or 02 to 04, who rolls off the screen or 03 to 02, who is cutting wide down outside lane 2.

Diagram 31 is similar to Diagram 30 except that the jumper 05 breaks off a screen by 04 to outside lane 3 for a pass from

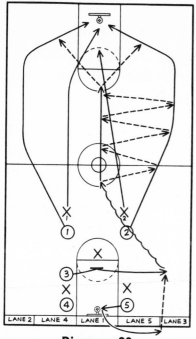

Diagram 28

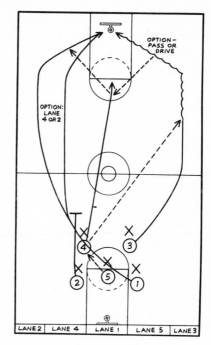

Diagram 29

Diagram 31

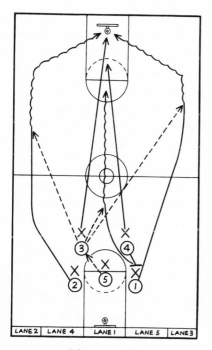

Diagram 30

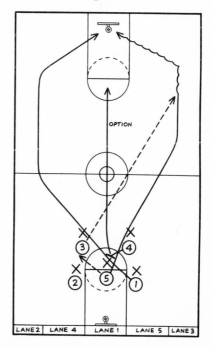

03 who receives the side tip from 05. 01 takes lane 2 off the screen by 04. 04 and 02 remain in the back court.

5. Other Fast Break Opportunities

The sixth inception point for the fast break is not as much a single point as it is a number of originating occurrences in which the fast break *team on defense recovers loose balls, steals the ball, or intercepts a pass* and quickly becomes an offensive threat. Previous discussion has been given to the application of defensive tactics whose purpose is to secure the ball prior to the field goal attempt, thus multiplying the opportunities for scoring. In fact, it is this purposeful action in any defense which is responsible to a great degree for the success of a team, regardless of the offense it employs.

In the remarks concerning complementing defenses (Chapter 3) it has been made clear that certain forms of defense are able to make the sixth inception group extremely potent in fast break scoring. The full-court, pressing defense, man-to-man, and zone defenses, with personnel applying alert anticipatory action, are those primarily recommended as applicable defenses to assist in originating the offensive. The defenses next in importance in this phase of fast break origin which is dependent on aggressiveness are the pressing defenses which concentrate their attack at the three-quarter and half-court areas.

Defenses of a third type include the 3-2 zone defense, the 2-1-2, the 2-3, and others. The 3-2 zone is especially effective since it is an overwhelming weapon against standard offenses involving one man or two men in the back court. The defense which is thrown at these offenses has the double-teaming technique with the intercepting potential and the immediate 3-on-2 or 3-on-1 offensive formation which is so sudden there is little or no possibility of defensive recovery by the victimized team (Diagram 32). In my opinion, the principal value of the 3-2 zone defense is in its relation to the indefensibility of its offensive possibilities. I have said before, "the zone defense is a good fast break offense."

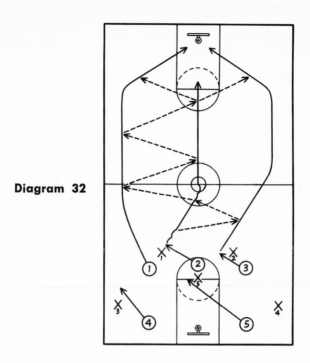

Diagram 32

The various points of inception which have been discussed are not automatically usable in the fast break offense. They must be activated. The inception points are available, and the players and teams who want to use them and who want to make their offense revolve around them may do so. The inception is only the beginning, but it is, of course, the basis for the total plan. I must repeat, the fast break is simple in its mechanics, but it takes a very great degree of individual and team determination to play this kind of game.

5

The Outlet Pass and
the Outlet Passer

A. THE OUTLET PASS

The outlet pass is the key to the continued development of
the opportunities offered by the principal point of inception.
The outlet pass releases the ball from the congested rebound
area out to the area of the court where the planned offense can
begin without pressure. All offenses, fast break included, make
use of this pass. However, the outlet pass utilized by the fast
break offensive is more clearly a decisive and definite phase of
the system. *The failure or success of the outlet pass being effectively completed determines the failure or success of the fast
break offense.* This is not the case in other offenses where the
defense's concentration on stopping the initial pass is either
absent or negligible (unless a pressing defense is being applied). The outlet pass in the fast break game is unique in that
it must be completed before the defense can defend against it.
Otherwise, it must be thrown to an area where the defense is
inadequate. Therefore, it must be sharp, and it must be de-
livered with speed. The best situation is one in which the outlet
pass receiver is in such a position when he receives the pass
that he forms part of a numerical advantage over the defense
at once.

48

L8					R8
L7					R7
L6	L5	L4	R4	R5	R6
L2	L3			R3	R2
L1		♙			R1

Diagram 33

The target area, the area to which the outlet pass is thrown, varies according to the reaction of the defense and according to the point of inception. Diagram 33 indicates the location of the various target areas in order of the best chance for success when the inception point is any one of the following:

a. Defensive rebound after a field goal attempt missed. Area 6, 5, 4, 3, 2. Right or left.
b. Defensive rebound after a free throw attempt missed. Area 7, 6, 5, 3, 2. Right or left.
c. End line throw-in after a field goal made. Area 8, 7, 6, 5, 3, 2. Right or left.
d. End line throw-in after a free throw made. Area 2, 3, 6. Right or left.

The outlet pass goes to the right or left target area, depending on the side of the goal or back board from which the ball rebounds and on which of the assigned defensive rebounders retrieves the ball and on the plan of attack in mind (coach's directions) in regard to the throw-in after the field goal or free throw made.

The target areas 4 and 5 to the right or left are often used by the outlet passer if there is a height advantage in his favor. If this is the situation, the defensive rebounder can clear the pass almost directly over the opposing offensive rebounders.

Target area 3 and 6 are the areas most likely to be free for the receiver. They are also located at an angle from the rebound triangle and, thus, able to be reached by passes from players who may be evenly matched in height.

49

Target areas 1 and 2 represent the points to which the rebound may be passed when the offensive rebounders have a big height advantage. They do not give the best down-court advantage however. On careful observation, it may be noted that the more difficult it is to release the outlet pass because of offensive rebounding opposition, the more laterally the pass is thrown. Area 1 is always open for the outlet pass. As the rebound is more frequently dominated by the defense, the farther removed from area 1 the outlet pass may be thrown. However, since the defensive back court men can on occasions intercept the outlet pass if it is thrown to deep areas 7 and 8, areas 3 and 6 are recommended as the best possible points of reception.

To further the success of the outlet pass when directed to a selected target area, the pass may be thrown from any place along the base line (according to the rules).

The deployment of players in the various target areas according to the best possibilities for successful pass completion is another one of the factors to be considered in the mechanics of the fast break offense.

B. THE OUTLET PASSER

Three players are responsible for the outlet pass. They are the three players who are assigned to the defensive rebounds. Regardless of the defense used, there is usually a three-man rebound triangle formed. Certain offenses require any three of five players to get the rebound; certain others designate the rebounders for all field goal attempts.

Requirements

The outlet passer needs the following characteristics:

Physical Characteristics

    a. Strong build
    b. Preferably tall
    c. The ability to jump
    d. Strong, quick hands

   e. Good speed in the running game

   f. Superior physical condition

   g. Agility and good coordination

Good Personal Characteristics

   a. Determination

   b. Aggressiveness

   c. Likes to "mix it"

   d. Refuses to quit

   e. Tireless in quest for victory

Other Requirements and Responsibilities

   a. He must have the ability and size or strength to block out opposing rebounders

   b. He must be able to rebound well from any one of the three rebound triangle points

   c. He must be able to throw the outlet pass to the receiver in any of the receiver's positions (Diagram 33) and in any and all fast break situations

   d. He must fill the lanes for the driving lay-up or short shot or fill the lanes for defensive back court coverage as the occasion demands

   e. He must crash the offensive boards for the follow-up rebound

   f. He must move well in the half court or set offense when the fast break is not successful

Added Skills Desirable

   a. The ability to skillfully execute the assortment of passes useful to the fast break offense:

      1. Baseball pass

      2. One-hand, bounce pass

      3. Hook pass

      4. Two-hand, overhead pass

      5. Lob pass

   b. The ability to pass with either hand, especially while in motion

c. The ability to shoot a fast, lay-up shot
d. A good sense of anticipation in regard to the position of the receivers
e. The ability to play a good free-lance game
f. The ability to shoot the intermediate shot well from the trailer position (18 to 24 feet from the goal)
g. The ability to play defense well

There are a few basketball players around who can qualify for the outlet passer's job. It is a big job, and unless the various foregoing responsibilities are divided between three rebounders, the comprehensive task may be too great for the average player. Fortunately, the fast break offense is so constructed that a player who can perform the main essentials of the operation can assist in its success. The essentials are the rebound and outlet pass.

Rebounding

The rebounder has as his objective the rebound *plus* the outlet pass. Consequently, his technique is slightly different. As he contacts the floor after his high leg-spreading rebound jump, he performs a half pivot away from the offensive rebounder (who is now on defense) toward the side line or base line and faces the side of the court toward which he plans to pass. He holds the ball away from the body, elbows slightly flexed for protection, and rotating it so the throwing hand is behind it and he can release the ball with the baseball pass instantly on sight of his free receiver. To do this, he may jump and pass or fake a jump and bounce pass the ball out. Either method of passing (or others which may be employed) calls for a pass which is sharp, fast, crisp.

The Pass

Some successful rebound pass-out players anticipate the possible receiving area of their teammate prior to the rebound so they can speed up the offense. They also use an inside back pivot as they hit the floor after securing the rebound. They face the contesting rebounder and pass the ball by him. Of course, the rebounder who has extra height or rebound jumping ability may jump high again after contacting the floor on securing the ball and use the two-hand or one-hand pass-out to clear the defenders.

When the rebounder contacts the floor with his side to the defender and his face to the side line to which he plans to pass, he may clear the release with the hook pass.

C. Progressive Drills for Developing the Outlet Passer and Pass Receiver

During the following progressive drills the emphasis is placed on the necessary fundamentals (see Chapter 8):

1. Blocking out the offensive rebounder.
2. One-hand "snatch" or two-hand "grab" rebounding.
3. Pivot step away or inside pivot for pass-out clearance.
4. Proper ball protection with body and arm extension combined with elbow flexion.
5. Ball rotation so the passing hand is behind the ball for the baseball pass.
6. The baseball outlet pass with speed and accuracy.
7. The follow-through to the proper lane after the pass has been completed.

The tremendous value of the outlet passer to a fast break team cannot be overestimated, nor can a coach spend too much time in developing this initial phase of the fast break offense. Particular attention must be given to the instructions on individual rebounding in Chapter 8. Get the ball! Get it out! Get going!

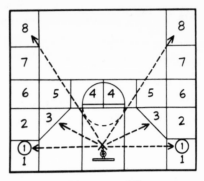

Diagram 34   **Diagram 35**

Drill 1

(Diagram 34.) Rebound pass-out and outlet-pass receiver's drill.

Skills to Be Developed:

1. Developing the outlet passer and his ability to rebound and throw the outlet pass quickly to a guard who is moving or has moved to the main pass-receiving area. Those passes are used which will clear a hypothetical defender.
2. Developing the skills of the outlet-pass receiver such as:
   a. Temporary block-out.
   b. Reaction to rebound position.
   c. Assumption of outlet-pass receiving position.
   d. Development of intermediate shooting (and follow up if desired).

Description of the Drill:

Stage One: The rebounder X3 positioned at the center of the foul circle. Guards (01) in a single line shoot individually from 18 to 24 feet radius with one guard X1 defending. His line is at the end of the court. X3 recovers the rebound. As the shot is in the air, the guard X1 follows up as far as the foul line. On determining which side of the goal the ball rebounds, he sprints to that side of the court, pivots, back to side line at the 6 outlet-pass receiving areas (Diagram 33), to receive the outlet pass from X3. X1 then goes to the rear of the shooting line. 01 goes to the rear of the defender's line. X3 continues re-

54

bounding through the entire line, then retires to give an opportunity to other rebounders.

Notes on the Drill:

When the ball rebounds to the left (as the shooter faces the goal), the defensive guard takes the outlet pass to his right.

When the ball rebounds to the right (as the shooter faces the goal), the defensive guard takes the outlet pass to his left.

When the ball rebounds to the center, the defensive guard takes the ball to his right.

When a field goal is made, the rebounder takes the ball out-of-bounds, makes two or three fast steps toward his right side line (as he faces the court), looks for his target planning a pass to by-pass a possible interceptor, passes the ball to the guard who has assumed a position along the side line for the throw-in.

Suggested Drill Progression:

Stage Two: An offensive rebounder (stationed in the top half of the circle) attempts to get the rebound from the 01 FGA and also attempts to prevent the outlet pass by tieing up X3 or blocking his pass.

Stage Three: Two rebounders versus two offensive rebounders.

Stage Four: Three defensive rebounders versus three offensive rebounders.

Stage Five: Three defensive rebounders and two guards on defense with two lines of shooters.

The above drills are *not* scrimmage drills.

Drill 2

(Diagram 35). Outlet pass drill for passing to various points of reception.

Skills to Be Developed:

1. The development of skills needed in passing the outlet pass

to the receiver at any one of the outlet-pass receiver's stations.

2. To teach the receiver the various positions to which the outlet pass may be thrown.
3. The development of the offensive rebounder's techniques in following up a shot, in tieing up a defensive rebounder, and in blocking the outlet pass.

Description of the Drill:

Stage One: A shooter makes a field goal attempt and X3 rebounds and passes to guard 01 at station 1 to 8 R or 02 at station 1 to 8 L. The pass-out is made according to the position in which the rebounder retrieves the ball, or from the end line if the field goal is made. The guards change stations on instruction from the coach. Assume a hypothetical defender in the choice of passes.

Notes on the Drill:

1. The pass-in after a field goal made always goes to the right (as the rebounder, now on offense, faces the court from outside the base line).
2. Interchange rebound positions during progressive drills.
3. Interchange the receiver's positions.
4. Mix the pass-receiving stations.

Suggested Drill Progression:

Stage Two: Use two rebounders passing out according to their rebound acquisition; same guard action.

Stage Three: Use three rebounders in the same manner; same guard action.

Stage Four: One defensive rebounder versus one offensive rebounder; same guard action.

Stage Five: Two defensive rebounders versus two offensive rebounders; same guard action.

Stage Six: Three defenders versus three offensive rebounders; same guard action.

Stages Seven to Thirteen: Repeat the drills in Stage One through Six, directing the guards to move from the center of the foul circle to designated stations after the field goal attempt.

D. THE OUTLET-PASS RECEIVER AND THE ALTERNATE PASS RECEIVER

The outlet-pass receiver is always one guard or the other. Either is the logical receiver since the center and forwards are engaged in the rebounding job. The receiver's position is noted in Diagram 33, where it is shown to vary from the corner and base-line area 1 to the center-line area 8 on the right and left sides of the court. The receiving position depends on the size and aggressiveness of the offensive rebounder and the skill, ability, and passing power of the defensive rebounder. As stated previously, the stronger the offensive rebounder's tactics, the closer to the base line the receiver positions himself; the weaker the offensive rebounder, the farther away from the base line the pass can be received. The wide range and latitude in pass reception open to guards is a strong recommendation for players who are fast and strong in maneuverability.

In my opinion, the qualifications, characteristics, and responsibilities of the guards who play in the fast break offense assure a permanent place in basketball for the "little man." This place should be open from the upper elementary school, right on through to the professional teams. The relatively small players manning the guard posts are extremely valuable in the many tactics involving the offensive development. If a coach thinks only defensively, he is worried about what will happen to his team and especially to his small guards when larger opponents have the ball. If he thinks offensively, he lets his opponents do the worrying when his team has the ball in its possession. It is quite unlikely that the larger defensive player can contain the small player. The superior mobility of the small guard in the wide-open game practically always offsets his doubted defensive prowess, if indeed it was ever a liability.

Except for rebounding, to which guards are not ordinarily assigned, the same tactics so effective offensively are applicable to defensive play. Such players cannot be cast aside simply on a height basis. Three tall rebounders and two small outlet-pass receivers, provided they have the speed, are ideal for the fast break offense.

Requirements

Following are the qualifications of the guard or outlet-pass receiver:

Physical Characteristics

   a. Strong, durable, can take contact.
   b. Smaller than the forwards and centers in size, but more agile, quicker, and speedier.
   c. Has above average coordination under fast-moving conditions.
   d. Demonstrates a well-conditioned physical status which can sustain him through a full-length game of full-court basketball featuring the pass and the fast break.
   e. Has a sense of anticipation of team ball possession which allows him to get a step ahead of the defense.

Personal Characteristics

   a. A strong desire to excel.
   b. A strong determination to execute responsibilities.
   c. A spirited "go-go-go" style.
   d. An aggressive, pressurizing approach to offense and defense.
   e. An attitude which defies fatigue.
   f. An attitude which cannot accept defeat. He refuses to give up.

Responsibilities

   a. Blocks out offensive guards going in for rebounds.
   b. Maneuvers position to receive the outlet pass. Gets in the clear and makes a good target.

"A good target" means that the guard, after his temporary blocking-out assignment, and after he anticipates or actually sees his rebounders secure the rebound, quickly moves to the free area on the side line and pivots in a direction in which he does not lose sight of the ball to a stationary position with his back parallel to the side line. In this position he can see the entire court and can determine the direction and type of move he will next make to receive the outlet pass. If the ball comes to him in the area he selects, he can simply rotate his body slightly for the pass reception; the foot position need not change. The receiving area most often open is Area 6, Diagram 35. It is very difficult for an opposing player to follow up on his offensive assignment and at the same time cover the receiver who moves to Area 6. Of course, the faster the pass-out and the finer the coordination there is between the passer and receiver, the better this position or any position will be.

The receiver must primarily take the back-to-the-side lines position (if only for an instant) in order to present a stationary target and thereby reduce the probability of errant passes. From such a position, he also sets up means by which he can escape an opposing guard who has been assigned to break up the outlet pass or who decides on his own initiative to stop the fast break at this point. If the opposing guard X1 goes for the cutoff, the outlet-pass receiver moves on the moment of commitment to Area 7 or 8 and takes the lob pass from 05 (Diagram 36). If X1 decides to go "behind" 01 and attack him im-

Diagram 36 **Diagram 37**

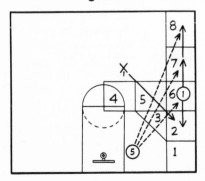
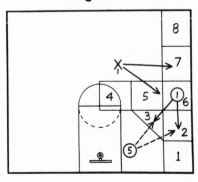

mediately after he (01) receives the pass, 01 moves forward at the moment of commitment to Area 3 (to Area 2 if the outlet pass is held up at the rebound zone, Diagram 37).

01 may move unimpeded down Lane 3 if X1 does not attack him in Area 6 or 7. If he does attack his possible progress route by playing Area 7, 01 may drive quickly (dribbling) to Lane 1. If X1 retreats to a back-court, defensive point, 01 may dribble Lane 1 (Diagram 38). The good outlet-pass receiver must be adept at these fast break coordinating techniques. (If he wishes to further his importance to his team, he should be made aware that the most valuable asset for fast-breaking guards is the ability to by-pass a single defender who is usually stationed in the middle of the court. The guard who can dribble, pass, or cut for pass reception past any one defensive player, giving the quick two-on-one or three-on-two situation, is "worth his weight in gold.")

On receiving the outlet pass, the receiver must, with split-second reaction, decide whether to pass to a teammate (depending on the circumstances), to dribble the side line or center lane, or whether to hold on to the ball, letting the initial fast break possibility go by and begin the secondary, set, offensive plan.

Since a coach is very often lucky to have *one* player who can excel in the responsibilities mentioned, it is not unusual to designate the guard who is to handle the outlet-pass reception regardless of where the outlet pass is to go. This means such a guard will operate from either the right or left pass-out areas. If this arrangement is considered, the coach must recognize the

Diagram 38	Diagram 39

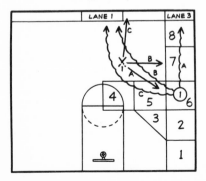

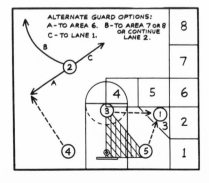

time limitation imposed on the outlet passer since he must wait for a "special" receiver. Furthermore, it will not take long for the defense to spot the fact that the receiver is always the same player, and there will be an increase in pressure tactics to contain him. However, by training the alternate guard in compensating action (acting as an alternate receiver or getting down court in order to depress the defense) and improving the better receiver's skill and increasing his repertoire of options, the defense's delaying action will be ineffective.

It should be noted that rebounds fall with greater frequency in the offensive left or center area. Therefore, 05 (Diagram 39) and 03 will be the most likely players to pass out to their offensive right. The better guard can be assigned to receive most passes in right Area 3, or either guard will take the ball at this point, whoever is closest to it. When the rebound is taken off the boards to the offensive right (usually by 03), the rebound pass out goes to left Area 3 to the assigned guard or to either guard, whoever can get to that point first.

E. The Alternate Pass Receiver

The opposite or alternate guard from the outlet-pass receiver has certain responsibilities which depend on the fast break plan in effect. In some instances, he will go to Lane 1 and receive the second pass from the outlet-receiving guard. In others, he will break down in Lane 1, 2, or 3, depending on the assignment given to him (Diagram 39). Accordingly, the action of the guard receiving the ball is dependent on the plan in use, as is the follow-up action of the entire team.

Since the outlet pass is the basic pass for fast break success and the outlet passer and outlet-pass receiver are the key men in the initial procedure toward fast break scoring, it is necessary for the skills involved to be practiced at length. The coach should stress drills and exercises designed to achieve the necessary, cooperative, coordinating action between passer and receiver.

6

The Third Man and the Trailers

A. THE THIRD MAN

The discussion thus far of the personnel of the fast break offense seems to indicate that each player is of equal importance to the success of the system. One of the reasons the fast break is such a great team game is that each player's part is quite as important as that of any of his teammates. Furthermore, each part is clearly seen as a direct factor in the mechanics of the whole system. The progression of techniques begins with the points of inception where the fast break is originated; then comes the outlet pass, with the maneuvers of the outlet-pass receiver to get numerical advantage at once; from this point, the down-court rush to fill the three lanes completes the sequence and leads to the ultimate aim—scoring.

The task of filling the third lane is the task of the third man. Which man on the team is the third man? He is actually any one of three men, any one of the three, defensive rebounders. Diagram 40 shows the beginning of the fast break and the players eligible to become the third man.

The sequence is as follows:

The rebound is taken off the defensive back board by one player in cooperative blocking-out action by three players.

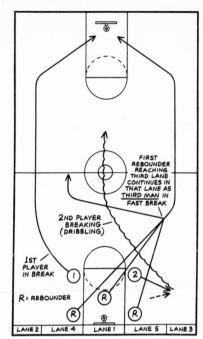

Diagram 40

FIRST
REBOUNDER
REACHING
THIRD LANE
CONTINUES IN
THAT LANE AS
THIRD MAN IN
FAST BREAK

2ND PLAYER
BREAKING
(DRIBBLING)

1ST
PLAYER
IN BREAK

R = REBOUNDER

LANE 2 | LANE 4 | LANE 1 | LANE 5 | LANE 3

The outlet pass is made from the defensive rebound by one player of three.

The outlet pass is received by one of two players.

Three lanes are to be occupied in the fast break attack which can be expected to work best against a normal defense.

Three lanes are to be occupied by three of five players.

The number-one man going down court is one of the guards, usually the guard who is not receiving the outlet pass. The number-two man down is usually the other guard after he receives the outlet pass. The third man in the third lane has been identified as one of the three rebounders. Further reducing the selection, the third man should be one of the two rebounders who is not engaged in actually grabbing the rebound. He may be a part of the rebound triangle, but when any one of the three secures the ball on the defensive rebound, the remaining two disengage themselves from the under-the-basket melee and race each other to the open lane. A good sense of anticipation in regard to the rebound and the outlet pass can assist the third man in "getting out and down." Occasionally, the position of players allows the outlet passer also to be the third lane man.

There are some fast break plans which call for one of the three rebounders to be the first man down-court. This fast break is somewhat less speedy than those where the guards go first, yet it is effective under circumstances where the opponent's rebounder is slow and unconditioned to a full-court attack. Diagram 41 shows how the third man becomes the number one or two man in the offense. The guard 02 in lane 3 receives the outlet pass; the guard 01 in lane 1 waits for the relay while lane 2 is quickly occupied by the third man 03. He causes the defense to retreat and thereby lessens the pressure on 01 in the center lane.

During a recent trip to Europe and Russia with a group of "U. S. All-Stars," our fast-breaking squad had a counter–fast-break thrown against them by one of the Russian teams (Diagram 42) in which the two rebounders who were not engaged in the rebound pass-out took the two outside lanes. The outlet

Diagram 41   **Diagram 42**

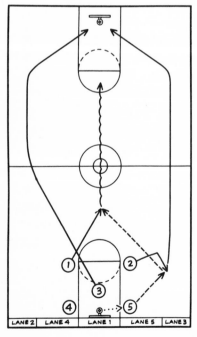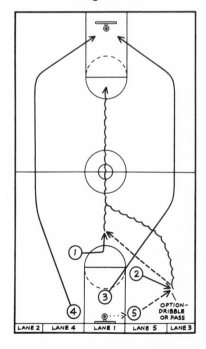

pass went to the Area 2 (Diagram 33) near the corner and side line to a guard 01, who dribbled up the side line, then to center lane 1. The outlet passer 05 and the alternate guard 02 followed the play in lanes 4 and 5. Several teams in the United States have been using a variation of this particular fast break plan for some time.

Regardless of whether one or both of the rebounders is the third man, second man, or first man down court, the significant thing is that the third lane is filled. The question of who is in the lanes is secondary to that fact.

We have already listed the desirable physical and personal characteristics for the outlet passer. They are the same for the third man, inasmuch as they are the same persons. Along with those qualifications, however, there should be listed "an understanding of the function of the third man in the third lane on the fast break."

I stated earlier that the third lane player is the key to fast break scoring. He is the key in the sense that the opponents should be depended on to have two men recover to a defensive position against a fast break team. There are two offensive men who are going fast, the two guards, but they must expect two defensive men to pick them up. If only one defender is in position, the 2-on-1 plan will be enough for the purposes of the offense. A third man will not be needed. Neither will he be needed if 01 or 02 is good enough to bypass one defender and bring about the 2-on-1. He certainly would not be needed if the fast outlet pass to one guard can be followed by a long, quick pass to the other guard who gets behind the defense for the solo lay-up. However, we must prepare for the worst and hope for the best. The whole matter breaks down into a single question which involves a single man. Can the third player on offense (who will form the 3-on-2 situation) move into position in the scoring area before the third defensive player can get back on defense and organize himself and his two teammates to stop the scoring possibility? An affirmative answer indicates the value of the third man. An affirmative answer indicates his determination to bring this phase of the fast break into fruition. The third man's function is dual: By occupying the third or open lane, he lessens the defensive pressure on each of the two players in the other two lanes. The faster he moves toward or into the optimum scoring area, the less the two defenders can do toward defending against his two teammates. When the third man drives in via the open lane, neither of the two defensive players can play any one of the three offensive players. They must play between players. They cannot commit themselves to defending any one or two players on offense without allowing a field goal to be made by one left free.

When your opponents have you outmanned in terms of size in the big rebounder department, and especially when they have that one extra large player who cannot or will not run, you may wish to assign the third lane to the player their big man is to cover. Your player is to fill the third lane after every rebound, after every field goal made, and after every free throw made or missed; the object being to "run the big man out of the game." If the "big man" takes a trailing player, use the four-lane fast break. Use the third man to put an embarrassing spotlight on the defensive performance of the opponents' big offensive threat.

Following are some of the drills used to develop the third-man aspect of the fast break:

1. "Little Man—Big Man" (Diagram 43)

A single line is formed out-of-bounds along the side line at the corner of the court. Each guard ("Little Man") with a ball has a forward or center ("Big Man") behind him. The guard dribbles the length of the court, shooting a right-hand lay-up or close shot. The forward who trails immediately behind him rebounds (if the shot is missed) and passes out to the guard, who has "taken off" after his shot down the right side line. If the shot is made, the guard will wait along the side line not farther than the mid-court line for the forward or center to take the ball out-of-bounds and baseball pass the ball to him. On receiving the ball, the guard then dribbles to the free-throw circle and passes off to the forward or center, who is driving in from the outside lane for a lay-up shot. The guard follows up to rebound or to recover the ball and take it off the court as a safety measure.

This drill may involve various techniques of passing and shooting at the return end of the court. The drill should be run from the opposite side of the court for left-hand lay-up practice and for the left-side pass out. Over a dozen pairs can be kept active if each will wait until the preceding pair crosses the mid-court line before following.

2. "Little Man—Big Man Plus One" (Diagram 44)

A third player, usually a forward, is placed behind the two forming the "Little Man—Big Man" duo. He is a defensive player who trails the two as they drive to the goal. He attempts (1) to offensively rebound the ball if the field goal attempt is

Diagram 43   **Diagram 44**

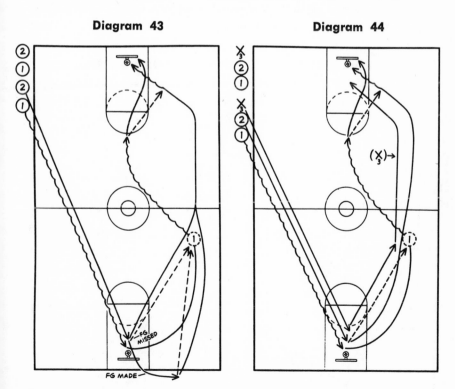

missed, (2) stop the outlet or inlet pass, and, finally, (3) he chases the two players, attempting to stop their 2-on-1 scoring as they return to the starting end of the court.

3. "Little Man—Big Man Plus Two" (Diagram 45)

A fourth player, usually a guard, lines up behind the three mentioned in Drill 2. As the dribbler begins his drive, the fourth player runs to the outlet-receiving area. The three players continue their actions as described in Drill 1 and 2, except that the shooter now continues his break down the right side line, and player 4 takes the outlet pass and dribbles to the foul circle. Player 2 goes to the opposite, side line lane. Player 4 now has the option of passing to Player 1 or 2, as Player 3 tries to break up a 3-on-1 attack.

4. "Little Man—Big Man Plus Three" (Diagram 46)

The action in Drill 3 is repeated, except a fifth player trails the shooter and rebounder or waits at mid-court in an effort to stop any phase of the fast break being practiced. This player may remain the same for several trials.

Diagram 45   **Diagram 46**

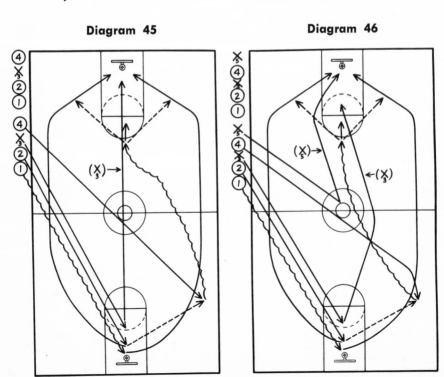

The foregoing drills involve many transferable elements of offense and defense which may confront a player who is to be the third man in the fast break offense. They further develop the center lane guard's drive, dribble, and pass-off skills and are excellent for conditioning purposes.

B. THE TRAILERS

Depending on the plan being used in a fast break attack, the players referred to as "the trailers" may be any two of the five members of the team. However, since at least one guard is always involved in the initial action, regardless of the idea being developed, and since there are three lanes which must be filled in the plan most likely to succeed, one of the trailers is always one of the rebounders. In the preceding notes on my own conception of the fast break offense, there are always two guards engaged in the three-lane, front-line attack, which leaves two of the original three rebounders as the trailing players. The guards are the first two men breaking, one rebounder is the third man, and the trailers are the remaining two rebounders, the fourth and fifth men, who form the second and follow-up "wave." These two second wave players are two of the three who tried to fill the third man spot but failed to do so simply because their teammate outsped them to the open lane.

An exception to the preceding statement is noted in cases where the trailers are specifically assigned to the third lane or to certain trailer responsibilities because of their particular qualifications.

It might be mentioned here that the ideal fast break is one in which the guard responsibilities are handled by either guard with equal effectiveness and where the abilities of the center and forwards are such that they can manage any position dictated by the circumstances. The assigned responsibility idea, however, represents a more realistic approach since such team versatility is rare.

Additional Requirements

The trailers (practically synonymous with rebounders) should possess the same physical and personal qualifications as those of the rebounders, mentioned in Chapter 8. They should, in addition, be able to manage the following assignments:

1. *Defend against the possible fast break counterattack of the opponents* by remaining near the mid-court area to which they have advanced as they trail the fast break of their teammates (Diagram 47).

The counter–fast-break is the fast break turned against a team which mishandles or badly passes the ball in the 2-on-1, 3-on-2 situations, allowing the defenders to intercept or recover the ball and immediately reverse the fast break with the numerical advantage on their side.

The trailers take a balance back-court, defensive position to combat this possibility. They maintain such a position until it is clear that their fast break is successful or unsuccessful, that a change to the secondary (set) offense will take place, or until the time for them to enter into other follow-up assignments.

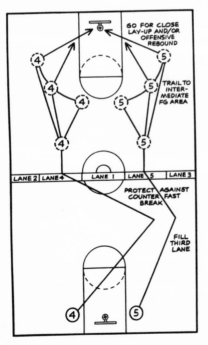

Diagram 47

2. *Trail the three players ahead to the intermediate shooting area for the intermediate field goal attempt* (Diagram 47). The field goal attempt quickly follows the realization that the defense has organized to stop the close-shooting aspect of the fast break.

The center lane guard, when confronted with three defenders between him, his two teammates, and the goal, brings the ball to a stop (at a position between the top of the circle and the foul line) and passes back to the free trailer, who has moved to a point from which he will make his field goal attempt. The pass to the trailer may be preceded by a back pivot (Diagram 47).

The use of a trailer for this unique type of attack usually requires a specifically assigned player, one with high-percentage accuracy from 21 to 25 feet out.

3. *Fill lane four or five, driving into the optimum scoring area* for a pass from the center lane guard or from an outside lane player in what becomes a 4-on-3 situation (Diagram 47).

The trailer in this assignment uses his speed, quickly breaking through the usually open lane. He does not lag behind here as he does in assignment 1 and 2. Precise ball-handling and passing are needed in this maneuver, because the back court is left with but one defender. The best defense against the return or counter–fast-break is to make good on the field goal attempt. This observation is applicable in all other fast break situations.

4. *Follow up the field goal attempt through lane four or five with strong offensive rebounding (Diagram 47).*

The trailer assigned to this task is usually selected for his particular ability in this technique. His secondary objective is to tie up the defensive rebounder to prevent the return fast break; in doing so, he allows the guard who is under the offensive board to return to the back court for his normal defensive or offensive duties.

On occasions, according to the coach's direction and according to the talents of the players, assignments three and four may be combined into a one-two maneuver.

5. *Participate in free-lance maneuvers* to follow up the fast break and/or move to assigned positions from which the secondary offense can begin.

Various techniques, other than those described in assignments 2, 3, and 4, may be added to the trailer's repertoire. Some may be free-lance, while others may represent a set or pattern movement designed to be an addition to the three-lane formation which has failed to give an advantage. Diagram 48 illustrates one such plan. The trailer 04 breaks on the baseline side of offensive players 02 and 03 in the outside lanes for a pass from the center-lane guard for a close shot.

Another technique which some coaches employ is the one in which one of the players ahead of the ball in either of the outside lanes, in a 3-on-3 situation, breaks quickly to a pivot spot and takes a pass from the middle man. The pivot gives off to a trailer breaking around to the vacated lane for the return pass and close shot. There is a lot to be said for this particular technique. It is a planned technique, however, as are most trailer plays. That is, the trailers and their maneuvers are used after planned practice and on directions from the coach. This is largely dependent on several important observations:

Who defenses the trailers, if anyone?

Are the trailers accurate shooters?

What are the offensive rebound opportunities when the trailers use the intermediate area for the undefended field goal attempt?

When teams play together for any length of time, many of the trailer plays are automatically sized up and reacted to on a free-lance basis, but without benefit of considerable experience the offense will devolve into a "run-and-shoot" affair. Unless there are explicit instructions given to the players in regard to their assignments, the controlled fast break will get out of control.

Other means of incorporating the trailers into the fast break plan will be mentioned in the following chapter on "The Free Lance Interim."

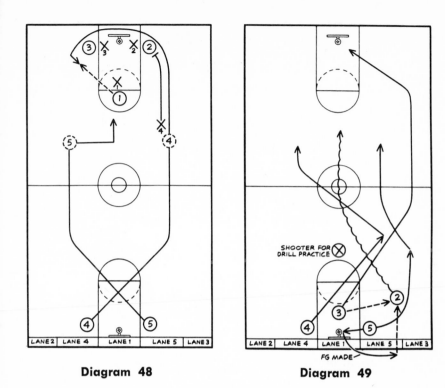

Diagram 48   **Diagram 49**

PROGRESSIVE DRILLS

Diagram 49

Skills to be developed:

Outlet passing and filling the third, fourth and fifth lanes quickly.

Description of the drill:

Three rebounders, 03, 04, 05, rebound and pass the outlet pass to a receiving guard, 01 or 02. One rebounder races to lane three, the other two trailing to lane four and five. A player shoots from various spots on the court. The end-line throw-in is practiced if the shot is successful.

Notes on the drill:

Practice passes which will clear a defender (offensive rebounder).

Emphasize speed in getting position in the lanes.

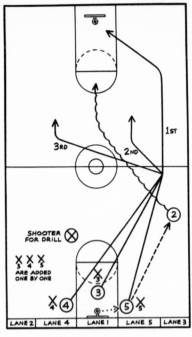

Diagram 50   **Diagram 51**

Suggested drill progression:

1. Add one offensive rebounder to the original drill. He works hard to get the offensive rebound, tie up the defensive rebounder, or otherwise delay or stop the outlet pass.
2. Add two offensive rebounders to the original drill.
3. Add three offensive rebounders to the original drill (Diagram 50).
4. Add to three offensive rebounders, one defender in the lane at the scoring end of the court.
5. Add two defenders to the above drill.
6. Add three defenders and use trailer options one to four; according to direction, first, and exercising options second. In this drill one of the offensive rebounders will "chase the play" only as far as mid-court (Diagram 51).

7

The Free-Lance Interim

When the defense adequately stops the fast break, the offense ordinarily resorts to a set or half-court plan with which to score. The offense then moves to various positions from which to begin its new attack. There are two distinct offensive ideas involved: (1) the fast break offense followed by (2) the set or half-court offense. Between these two ideas there is a period of time during which individuals or teams can take advantage of the lack of organized defense to score, using any one of many free-lance methods. I refer to this phase of the game as the "free-lance interim."

Free lance in this context refers to those offensive maneuvers which are not necessarily a part of a prepared pattern or plan but, rather, are the answer to a situation where an individual (or two individuals, or sometimes three individuals) sees an advantage which can be used for scoring without waiting for the total, preplanned team play idea to be effected. In my opinion, the mechanics of free-lance maneuvering can be and should be taught. When to employ any one or several of these maneuvers (they must be put into use automatically) at the moment of greatest advantage is something which requires many hours of playing experience. Learning the free-lance moves involving individual, dual, and three-man play is one thing; applying them to game situations is another.

Some examples of free lancing can be seen in the previous chapter on the trailer play of the fourth and fifth man in the fast break. In these instances the fast break is supposedly stopped (since the defenders are equal to the offenders); yet, before the team resorts to its secondary offense, there is a continuation of play which produces an opportunity to score. This continuation of play may be planned or it may result from the imagination and resourcefulness of players who seize an advantage and pursue it to a satisfactory conclusion.

It should be stated here that a happy balance must be sought between the preplanned team offense and non-planned, free-lance play. An all free-lance offense may result in chaos, but completely patterned or preplanned plays overlook individual initiative and its rewarding expression. A clear departure for a short period such as the brief free-lance interim is desirable, but there is a phase of play which arrives which must be recognized as the time to return to an organized, team-play idea.

Needless to say, quick thinking, quick, coordinated action in passing, cutting, and screening by the center guard are of utmost importance in fast-moving, free-lance play. This player has the ball most of the time when the fast break's first attack is momentarily halted. He is the originator, then, of most of the follow-up moves where a continuation of play is recommended rather than a complete breakdown in game continuity while the set offensive formation is assumed.

Diagram 52 shows a follow-up maneuver where 01, the center guard, seeing three defenders between him and his two teammates and the goal, passes to 02 and screens for 03, who cuts off the screen for the pass from 02 and a close FGA. This maneuver, of course, can go to either side.

Diagram 53 illustrates a pass from 01 to 02 who passes off to 01 after 01 fakes a cut to the opposite side of the lane but cuts off 02 for the shot. 02 may assist in the action by moving slightly away from X2 to make the pass and cut by 01 more effective.

Diagram 54 shows 01 dribbling off to the right (or left) of the center lane and screening X2 (or X3) out of the hand-off to 02 (or 03). Such a maneuver occurs as quickly as 01 senses that the defense is equal to the offense (3-on-3). Diagram 55 is a similar maneuver except that 01 passes off to either 02 or 03 and follows the ball, screening X2 (or X3) for 02 (or 03) to move off the screen for the field goal attempt.

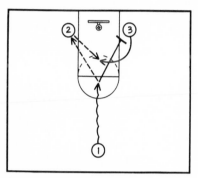

Diagram 52

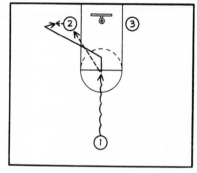

Diagram 53

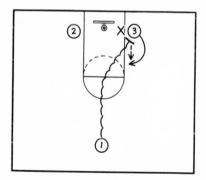

Diagram 54

Diagram 55

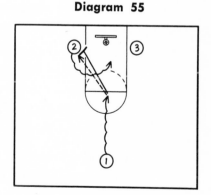

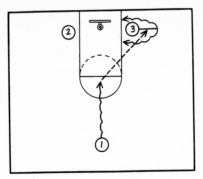

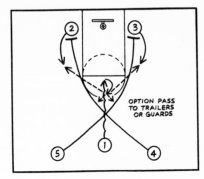

| Diagram 56 | Diagram 57 |

In Diagram 56 03 quickly backs out of his position, receiving the pass from 01. He shoots or fakes a shot and drives the base line or around X3, depending on X3's reaction.

Diagram 57 has 01 pivoting, and 04 and 05 crossing and going in for a close shot if either receives the pass-off. If neither receives the pass-off, they both screen for 02 and 03 who break off the screen for the pass and shot.

The above maneuvers may be executed on the personal initiative of any one player. Reaction is the key—reaction to the moves of one player by an answering move of another. If these ingredients are missing in the players, the best thing to do after the fast break breaks down is to withhold the ball from any offensive act, skip the free lance, and proceed carefully to the secondary offense.

In keeping with my belief that free-lance moves should be taught, there follow fifteen free-lance maneuvers involving one offensive player versus one defensive player. These moves are also preliminary to two-versus-two and three-versus-three free-lance techniques:

ONE-VERSUS-ONE MANEUVERS

Diagram No.	Description	Instruction and Comment
58	Right Dribble Around Defense	When a defensive player is out of position to the offensive player's left, the offensive player quickly moves the ball to his right hand, then steps off with the left foot

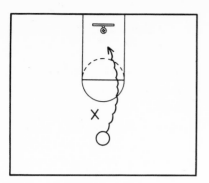

Diagram 58

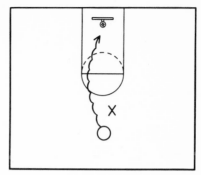

Diagram 59

Diagram No.	Description	Instruction and Comment
		in a long, low step, beginning his dribble with the right hand and continuing his driving dribble to the goal for one of the seven, basic, lay-up shots. In the initial step get the shoulders by the defense's body if possible. Keep the ball to the outside in the dribble. Use speed!
59	Left Dribble Around Defense	Reverse procedure used in Diagram 58.
60	Single Fake Right	Assuming the defense is in good position, a fake or feint must be used to make the defense move, losing position or balance. Fake right, using a fast step forward and outside the defense's position. Quickly recover and dribble to left using technique as in No. 48. On the fake move the ball to the outside; on the reverse to the left, shift the ball to the left or outside hand. Make this move stronger by using shoulders, head, eyes. Use speed!

Diagram 60

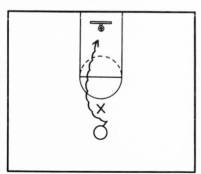

79

Diagram No.	*Description*	*Instruction and Comment*
61	Single Fake Left	Reverse procedure used in Diagram 60.
62	Double Fake, Left, then Right	Employ a fake to left, recover, fake to right, then drive to left using tactics outlined in Diagram 58 and Diagram 60. Make each fake convincing.
63	Double Fake, Right, then Left	Reverse procedure used in Diagram 62. Continue with tactics suggested in Diagrams 58, 60 and 62.
64	Back Half-Pivot Left	From a parallel stance facing the defense, quickly half-pivot left with a long, low step to the outside of the defense, moving ball to the left hand for beginning the

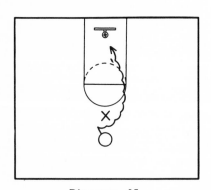

Diagram 61

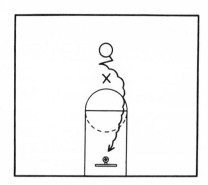

Diagram 62

Diagram 63

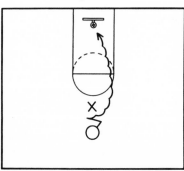

Diagram
No.   *Description*   *Instruction and Comment*

dribble. Avoid contact on the
pivot. Drive off the pivot on right
foot toward the goal. Continue as
in No. 58, 60.

65   Back Half—   Reverse procedure used in Dia-
        Pivot Right   gram 64.

66   Full Front   From a stride stance when at-
        Pivot (Left or   tacked by the defense, pivot with
        Right Foot in   front of body leading to a reverse
        Back-Pivot   position. If the defense attacks to
        Position)   the rear, quickly continue the
                                pivot to the front in a complete
                                or full pivot move, shifting ball to
                                the outside hand for a low, fast
                                drive and dribble. Avoid charging
                                foul. Keep pivot foot in one spot.

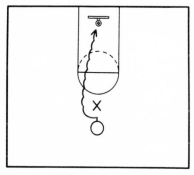

Diagram 64

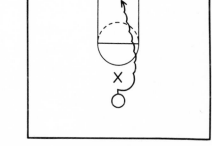

Diagram 65

Diagram 66

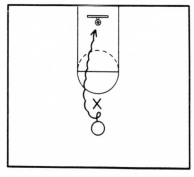

Diagram

No.	*Description*	*Instruction and Comment*
67	Full Back Pivot (Left or Right Foot in Back-Pivot Position)	From a stride stance when attacked by the defense, pivot with the rear of the body leading to a reverse position. If the defense attacks to the front of the body, quickly continue the pivot in a complete or full pivot move, shifting the ball to the outside hand for a low, fast drive and dribble to the goal.
68	Fake Right— Step Back	Very often during a strong, convincing feint by the offense, the defensive player will step back but otherwise maintain his position in line with the goal he is defending; the offensive player may then employ a fake forward to right, and if the defense moves back, the offense returns to his original position and shoots over the defense with a one hand or two hand set shot or a jump shot. If the offensive player needs more space for his shot, he may retreat a further step by dribbling once as he moves backward to his shooting position. This technique is especially applicable in the close and intermediate shooting areas. Do not move the pivot foot as the fake is employed.

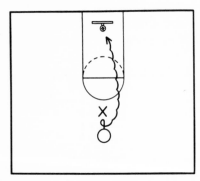

Diagram 67

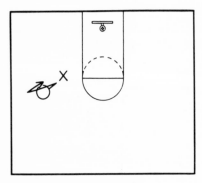

Diagram 68

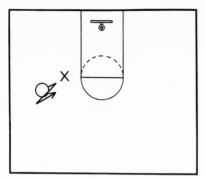

Diagram 69

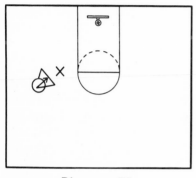

Diagram 71

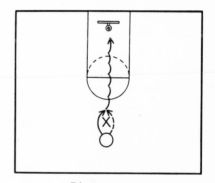

Diagram 70

Diagram 72

Diagram No.	Description	Instruction and Comment
69	Fake Left— Step Back	Same as Diagram 68 except initial fake step is to the left.
70	Double Fake, Right, Left, Step Back	Same as Diagram 68 except double fake with initial step to the right.
71	Double Fake, Left, Right, Step Back	Same as Diagram 68 except double fake with initial step to the left.
72	Air Dribble	A surprise move which is usable occasionally is the Air Dribble ("An air dribble is that part of a dribble during which the dribbler throws or taps the ball in the air and then touches it before it touches the floor"—*N.B.C. Rule Book.*) As the defense steps close

83

Diagram No.	*Description*	*Instruction and Comment*
72 (*cont.*)		to the offensive player, the offensive player quickly tosses the ball over the head of the defensive player and quickly circles outside and around him to (1) catch the ball with both hands and shoot or pass or (2) let the ball bounce from the floor and initiate a regular dribble from the first contact. If two hands are placed on the ball or the ball comes to rest in one hand or two hands, the dribble ends.

Many of the above techniques may also be employed to gain an improved position for passing or scoring by a player *without* the ball.

Two-versus-Two Maneuvers

Two-versus-two maneuvers form the basis for two-versus-two free-lancing and are too numerous and varied to enumerate;

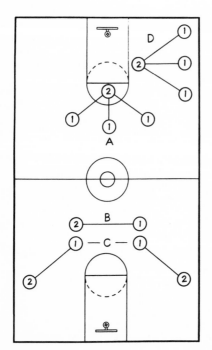

Diagram 73

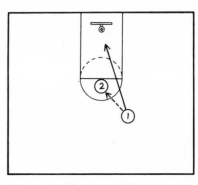

Diagram 74

however, the following diagrams represent some of these techniques. In any two-man play situation the players may be spatially related to each other by the positions noted in Diagram 73.

Guard to center, illustrated by A.

Guard to guard, illustrated by B.

Guard to forward, illustrated by C.

Forward to center, illustrated by D.

Diagram

No.	Description	Instruction and Comment
74	Guard to center or forward to center pass (73 A-D). Pass and cut for return pass using only speed to advantage.	01 faces 02 (who has back to basket) and, using any one of a variety of into-the-pivot passes, gets the ball into the center; 01 then cuts fast for a return pass (direct or bounce) from 02.
75	Pass and cut for return pass after single fake (right and left).	Same as 74 except the cut to the left by 01 is preceded by a single fake to the right or by a fake to the right and a cut to the left.
76	The player passes and cuts for return pass after double fake (right and left).	Same as 74 except the cut to the left by 01 is preceded by a double fake by 01 left-right-left cut or right-left-right cut.

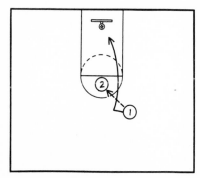

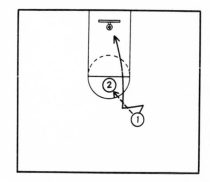

Diagram 75   **Diagram 76**

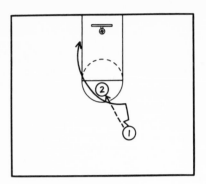

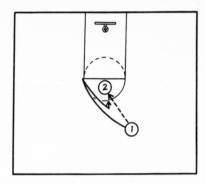

Diagram 77　　　　　　　　**Diagram 78**

Diagram No.	*Description*	*Instruction and Comment*
77	The player cuts after his pass in (and single or double fake) and changes direction (right and left).	When player 01 starts his cut, the defense may play him well or overplay him to the cut side; the player then changes direction and gets the return pass to the opposite side from which he was originally cutting.
78	The player cuts and reverses back out (right and left).	The player 01 passes the ball into the pivot man 02, cuts by and reverses back out leaving his guard behind the post and then receiving the pass from the center for a shot over the top or a drive-in move.
79	The player cuts by and receives pass after fake hand-off and dribble to opposite side (right and left).	Player 01 cuts by and receives a fake return pass then the actual pass as the pivot man 02 dribbles opposite the fake *then* passes to the cutter.

Diagram 79　　　　　　　　**Diagram 80**

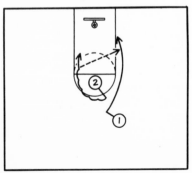

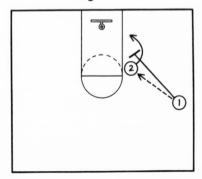

Diagram
No.   *Description*   *Instruction and Comment*

80   The player passes   Player 01 passes in to the pivot
      and sets a screen   player, 02, follows the ball and
      for the receiver   sets a screen to the inside of
      (right and left).   player 02 for 02 to dribble behind
                               and shoot.

81   The player dribbles   01 dribbles his defensive man into
      his defensive man   the post 02 for a rub-off and con-
      into the post man   tinues into scoring position. 02
      (right and left).   holds his position.

82   The player dribbles   Same as 81 except 02 rolls in for
      his defensive man   a pass from 01.
      into the post man,
      who rolls in for a
      pass.

83   "Blind" screen and   02 moves into X1 (who is guard-
      roll by pivot man   ing 01) for a rear or "blind"
      on guard's defense   screen. 02 rolls in after cut by 01.
      or by forward on
      guard's defense.

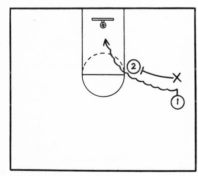

Diagram 81

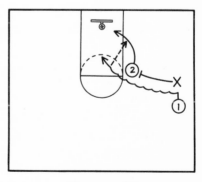

Diagram 82

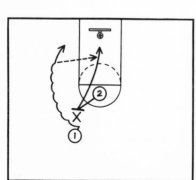

Diagram 83

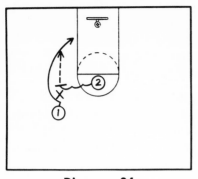

Diagram 84

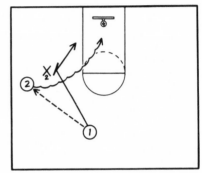

Diagram 85

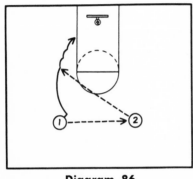

Diagram 86

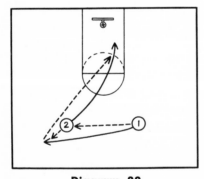

Diagram 87

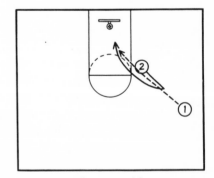

Diagram 88

Diagram 89

Diagram No.	Description	Instruction and Comment
84	Screen by man with the ball.	02 with ball dribbles to a screen position on 01 who cuts off the post for return pass.
85	Guard-to-guard passes (73 B-C). Pass and cut toward the receiver.	01 passes to 02 then follows, trying to get in front of his defender for the return pass. His cut may be preceded by a single or double fake.

Diagram

No.	*Description*	*Instruction and Comment*
86	Pass and cut away from the receiver.	01 passes to 02, fakes inside then cuts away from the ball in an effort to get X1 to turn his back on the ball and thus allow the old "dead slick" pass.
87	Pass and screen for receiver to dribble.	01 passes to 02, following to screen out X2. 02 dribbles off screen to right or left, depending on the position used for the screen.
88	Pass and go behind receiver for return pass.	01 passes to 02 and goes behind 02 for a return pass with 02 cutting for a return pass.
89	Fake reception and cut away.	02 fakes a reception from 01 then cuts.

THREE-VERSUS-THREE MANEUVERS

Free-lance basketball seldom involves more than three offensive players versus three defensive players. In fact, most pattern games engage only three players on one play or a revolving of three players within five most of the playing time. Following, are a few of the almost endless maneuvers in which

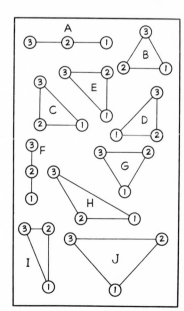

Diagram 90

three men can operate. These alignments form a part of practically every offense. (See alignments, Diagram 90)

Diagram
   No.   *Description*   *Instruction and Comment*

Note: "A," "B," "C," etc., refer to alignment of players as indicated in Diagram 90.

91(A)	(89A) Forward cut off 02 by 03 for pass from opposite forward 01, reverse; 03 pass to 01 cutting off 02.	03's cut off 02 should be preceded by a single fake or a double fake to assist in running X3 into the 02 post.
92(A)	Reverse screen.	When 01 receives the ball, 02 moves away from the ball to screen for 03 who cuts for a pass from 01. 03 may cut over or under 02 depending on screen position and X3's reaction.
93(B)	The cross play.	03 is usually positioned with his back to the goal. 03 receives the ball for a pass-off to 01 or 02 who cross on the cut. The player preceding may or may not be the player to pass the ball to 03. A bounce pass is used after the cutter moves to a lateral area on his cut.
94(B)	Screen and cross.	01 passes to 03 then screens for 02 who cuts. 01 screen-rolls in. 03 passes to 01 or 02. Reverse the play with 02 passing to 03.
95(B)	Pivotman's Rear Screen.	01 passes to 02 cutting off 03's rear screen on X2. Reverse play.

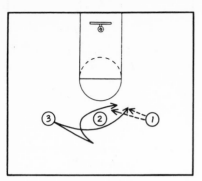

Diagram 91

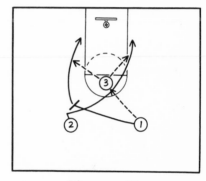

Diagram 92

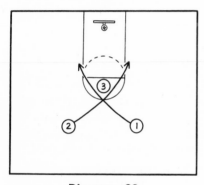

Diagram 93

Diagram 94

Diagram No.	Description	Instruction and Comment
96(B)	Fake cross.	01 passes to 03 and begins cross but stops. 02 fakes cross and cuts off 01 for pass from 03. 01 continues cut to basket after screen. Reverse play.

Diagram 95

Diagram 96

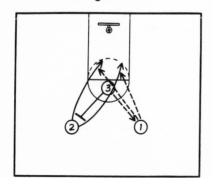

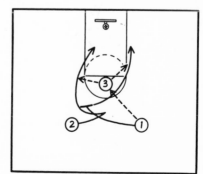

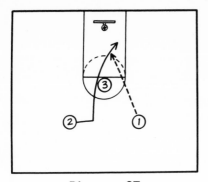

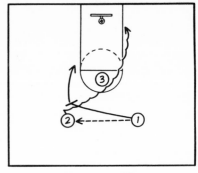

Diagram 97   **Diagram 98**

Diagram No.	Description	Instruction and Comment
97(B)	Cut off the post.	01 passes to 02 who cuts off the post 03 after fake in. Cut can go over or under post or can work in reverse by pass to 01 from 02.
98(B)	Dribble off screen and post.	01 passes to 02 and screens X2 for dribble in by 02 off 01 screen and 03 post. Reverse play. Option: 01 rolls after screen splitting post. Option: 03 rolls in after screen.
99(C)	Pass and cut off high post.	01 passes to 03 and cuts off 02 for pass from 03. 02 moves in for option pass from 03.
100(D)	Reverse of 99C.	
101(C)	Pass and cut off low post.	01 passes to 02 and cuts off 03 for pass from 02.
102(D)	Reverse of 101C.	

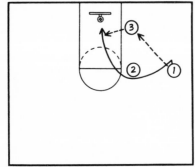

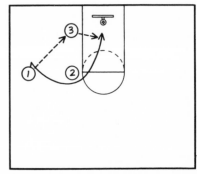

Diagram 99   **Diagram 100**

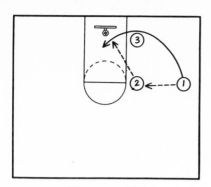

Diagram 101

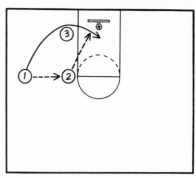

Diagram 102

Diagram No.	Description	Instruction and Comment
103(C)	Pass high, screen low.	01 passes to 02 and screens for 03 to receive pass from 02.
104(D)	Reverse of 103C.	
105(C)	Pass low, screen high.	01 passes to 03 and screens for 02 to receive pass from 03.
106(D)	Reverse of 105C.	

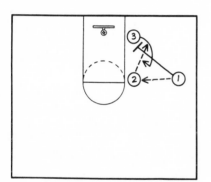

Diagram 103

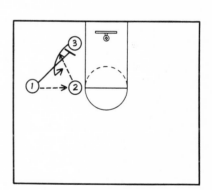

Diagram 104

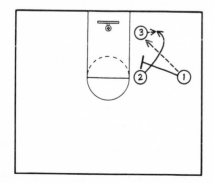

Diagram 105

Diagram 106

Diagram No.	Description	Instruction and Comment
107(E)	Guard pass, screen forward.	01 passes to 02, screens for 03 to cut for pass from 02. 01 screens and rolls in for option pass.
108(E)	Forward pass and screen guard.	03 passes to 02, screens for 01 who cuts for pass from 02. 03 screen rolls in for option pass.
109(E)	Lateral screen by pivot man.	02 screens X3 for 03 to cut for pass from 01.
110(E)	Guard cut off post.	01 cuts off 02 post for pass from 03.
111(E)	Forward cut off post.	03 cuts off 02 post for pass from 01.
112(F)	Dribble off high-low post.	01 dribbles off 02 and 03.

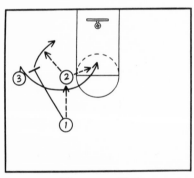

Diagram 107

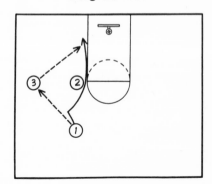

Diagram 108

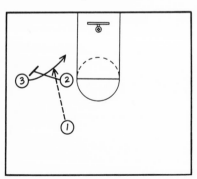

Diagram 109

Diagram 110

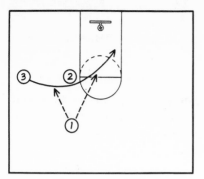

Diagram 111   **Diagram 112**

Diagram No.	Description	Instruction and Comment
113(F)	Low post to high pass.	03 moves off 02 and 01 for pass from 01.
114(G)	Pass and cut off either post.	Twin post offense with 02 and 03 as alternate pivot men. 01 passes to 03 and cuts off 02 for pass from 03.
115(G)	Pass and moving screen for alternate pivot man.	01 passes to 02, cuts between 02 and 03. 03 cuts off moving screen of 01 for pass from 02. Reverse play to opposite side.

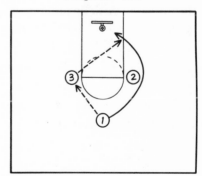

Diagram 114

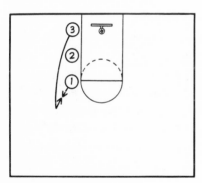

Diagram 113

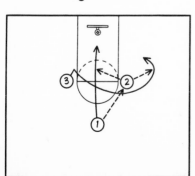

Diagram 115

Diagram No.	*Description*	*Instruction and Comment*
116(G)	Pass and set screen for alternate pivot man.	01 passes to 02, moves to screen for 03, who cuts off screen for pass from 02. Reverse play to opposite side.

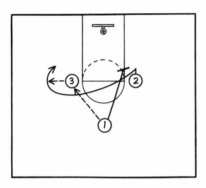

Diagram 116

The series of plays involving H, I, J are essentially the same as C, E, and G respectively, only the spacing is different.

Players should be taught the 1-on-1 moves first. The 2-on-2 maneuvers are based on practically all the 1-on-1 maneuvers with an added layer to work with, a player without the ball who serves to increase the defensive problem. With the proper learning of two-man play, the three-man moves are finally brought in. Ardent practice of the various ideas presented will soon have the players reacting to each other on cues and signals which are hardly apparent and which are based mainly on recognition of situations initiated by any one of the two or three players involved. This is free-lance basketball, and the "free-lance interim" is one phase of the game where its value can be appreciated.

8

Individual Fundamentals and Drills for the Offense

Fast break fundamentals are the fundamentals of basketball accelerated and modified. They are the same basics but with speed added. Consequently, they must be taught soundly, emphasized, and re-emphasized to the point where the addition of speed to action and execution does not affect efficiency.

A coach never wastes time if he works on fundamentals, for he must always return to them whenever he gets in difficulty. When considering the why of losing a game or games, he will come up with any number of reasons, but, usually, one or more aspects of the problem will be associated with fundamentals. Most of the time he can trace the problem to a lack of adequate training in fundamentals, a lack of concentration on fundamentals, or an omission of fundamentals. The fundamentals of basketball are the same wherever the game is played. The method of teaching them is different from coach to coach; the means, the degree of emphasis, the insistence on detail, are other variables. The variables determine the extent to which the fundamentals become interesting, challenging, rewarding, and actually learned.

It is not my intention to make fast break basketball seem so specialized that it might be considered a different game altogether. On the other hand, I believe there is some merit in presenting my own version of basketball fundamentals with emphasis on those which can be adapted to and modified for fast break offense.

The following fundamentals represent the skills which must be properly learned, practiced with determination and regularity, and executed with confidence if a player plans to become an above-average performer:

BASIC BASKETBALL AND FUNDAMENTALS OF OFFENSE

Fundamental Skills to be Learned	*Fundamentals and the Fast Break: Modifications, Methods, Comments*
1. Handling the Ball	
a. Handle the ball with the fingers.	a. Handling the ball with the fingers must be highly emphasized.
b. Palms of the hand never touch the ball during handling, passing, receiving, dribbling, or shooting.	b. This skill must be *thoroughly* learned. Most of the traveling violations occurring in a game originate from the inability of the player to receive, handle, and release the ball with the fingers only. High-speed ball-handling in the fast break cannot be accomplished if this fundamental is not *mastered.*
2. Static Passing (From stationary positions)	
a. Pass the ball using the fingers.	a. Passes must be quickly released without a long preparatory action (no big "wind-up" or telegraphing).
b. Use a pass which is easily receivable.	
c. Pass to the waist-to-shoulders area.	c. Pass the ball to the area of the shoulders.

Fundamental Skills to be Learned	*Fundamentals and the Fast Break: Modifications, Methods, Comments*
d. Do not spin the pass.	d. Learn the long pass without a spin or curve.

e. Learn a pass for each situation:
  1. Chest pass
  2. Baseball or overhand pass
  3. Softball or underhand pass
  4. Overhead pass
  5. Hook pass
  6. Bounce pass
	e. Pass the ball with speed. Straight-line passes are picked off. Emphasize the baseball pass and concentrate on distances of 40 to 50 feet. Revive the hook pass for passing out after rebounds. Spend time on the long one-hand bounce pass of distances of 40 to 50 feet or more. Use plenty of "steam" on the ball. The bounce pass for close, fast play in the scoring area is one of the necessary passes for the fast break. It is usually the pass which is made to the outside lanes from the center lane to the player who makes the driving lay-up. *Practice this pass!* It is *the* pass to use to bypass either retreating defenders or those who are already stationed in the scoring area.

3. Dynamic Passing
(Passing while in motion)

a. Players must be taught to pass the ball as they move naturally. Their running style does not change as running and passing are combined.	a. Concentrate on speed passing and running. Learn passing accuracy with speed drills involving several players in passing formations. Fingertip control eliminates turnovers via the traveling violation.

Fundamental Skills to be Learned	*Fundamentals and the Fast Break: Modifications, Methods, Comments*
b. Speed judgment must be learned. Judging the speed of a teammate and lead-passing to him without his losing stride.	
c. Pass and receive the ball with the fingers.	
d. Concentrate on accuracy.	d. Poor passes waste time and cause the loss of the needed step ahead of the defense. Accuracy must be stressed.
e. Do not pass a spinning ball.	
f. Avoid violating the traveling rule.	

4. Dribbling

a. Flex the trunk and legs slightly.	a. Speed dribbling is best accomplished from a semi-flexed position of the body and good balance for quick change of position.
b. Use a flexible wrist, fingers on the ball and forearm presure. Do not use the entire arm. No pumping or striking the ball.	
c. Place fingers on the ball. "Hands off!"	c. Exercise control over the ball with finger pressure.
d. Dribble with lower peripheral vision only; head up, eyes forward.	d. The ball is dribbled more to the front and waist-high in the fast-break, speed technique. Peripheral or split vision is an absolute *must*.
e. Learn various kinds of dribbling techniques and their	e. Add speed to the dribbling techniques.

*Fundamental Skills
to be Learned*

*Fundamentals and the
Fast Break: Modifications,
Methods, Comments*

uses, such as stopping and starting, turning, changing hands, changing directions, change of pace.

f. Precede dribbling with feinting (faking) left, right, double feints.

f. Practice the feints without violation of the rules in regard to foot position.

5. Combined Dribbling, Passing, Pivoting

a. Practice good footwork to avoid loss of ball from the traveling violation. Learn the rule on traveling from the rule book and teach the fundamentals accordingly.

a. Add speed and avoid loss of ball.

b. Practice the proper execution of the various pivot steps from a stride and square stance and from a stationary and moving position. Consult the rule book on the pivot steps.
Pivots:
Square stance:
Half and full pivots, right and left.
Stride stance:
Half and full pivots, right and left.

b. The addition of the preliminary feint or double feint (preceding the dribble) is often the move which gives the numerical advantage in the optimum scoring area to the offense. It is this practiced maneuver which allows the dribbler and the cutter to gain the one step ahead of the defense they need for improved scoring possibilities.

c. Practice the fake dribble, pivot-pass, and cut in one complete exercise. It represents an integral phase of all games.

c. The fake, pivot, and drive without the ball is a freeing move for the offensive player which places him in position for:
1. Better reception of the pass.
2. Better rebounding position offensively.

Fundamental Skills
to be Learned

Fundamentals and the
Fast Break: Modifications,
Methods, Comments

3. Better position in the lanes during the advantage of 3-on-2, 2-on-1, etc.

Utilize the head, feet, shoulders, eyes, body, in the fakes. Speed it up!

d. Without the ball, feint, pivot, cut.

6. Close or Lay-up Shooting

So much of the success of the fast break is dependent on the good, close shooting game. In the first place, you get the high percentage field goal attempt. The player should make the goal on his drive-in move or get fouled in the attempt. The more often he is on the foul line, the more valuable he is to the team.

a. Take off on the foot opposite the shooting hand.

a. As an option only, learn to shoot off the opposite or "wrong" foot.

b. Jump as high as possible, extending the shooting arm.

b. Avoid the "floating" shot. Jump high instead of long.

c. Keep the ball in both hands as long as possible, taking it to its highest point before continuing the shooting motion with one hand at the last moment before release.

c. Avoid spinning the ball on the fast lay-up. Shoot a soft, "dead" ball.

d. Practice the lay-up from varied angles, short distances, and varying speeds.

*Fundamental Skills
to be Learned*

*Fundamentals and the
Fast Break: Modifications,
Methods, Comments*

e. Precede the drive for the goal with foot, shoulder, and head fakes (with and without the ball).

e. Improve the faking to perfection, avoiding the loss of ball by violation.

f. Lay-up a soft shot regardless of the speed of the driver. The harder you drive, the softer the shot.

g. Learn, practice, and know when to use the seven basic lay-up shots as follows:
   1. Right side—right hand.
   2. Left side—left hand.
   3. Right side, going under the goal and shooting back over head with right hand, left hand, or both hands.
   4. Left side, going under the goal and shooting back over head with left hand, right hand, or both hands.
   5. Right side, going across to left in front of goal, shooting with left hand.
   6. Left side, going across to right in front of goal, shooting with right hand.
   7. Center shot, down the center and over the rim or shoot to the backboard for the bank-in shot.

g. The seven, basic, lay-up shots are usually as extensive a repertoire as will be needed to get a shot off against defensive problems presented to the player. Full speed, driving shots are a trademark of successful fast break teams. Combine the practice of these close shots with a long, hard dribble or with a bounce pass to the shooter from various positions from the top of the circle to the foul line. Unless a fast break team can shoot the lay-up accurately, it may be caught with insufficient forces to its rear to stop the same kind of attack coming back at them. The goal must be made; the time between the goal being made and the time it takes to get the ball into play from behind the end line is the time available to assume a good defensive position. Try for 90 to 100 per cent accuracy in lay-up shooting.

*Fundamental Skills
to be Learned*

*Fundamentals and the
Fast Break: Modifications,
Methods, Comments*

7. Intermediate Shooting
(12 to 22 feet)

a. Select the best shot and develop it.

b. Develop one good shot before attempting variations.

c. Determine the best distance for consistently accurate shooting.

d. In early developments, vary the distance and the position.

e. Practice shooting from a received pass if possible or off a short dribble.

f. Add the rebound follow-up to to the field goal attempt follow-through.

g. *Try to make every shot you attempt!*

The only modification in intermediate shooting for purposes of the fast break offense would be to have the player in motion as he assumes an intermediate shooting position from a previous spot, since shooting the ball on the move from a short, sharp pass will more closely approximate game conditions.

Very often, the intermediate shot is taken at the end of the fast break attack. It is open almost 100 per cent of the time.

Using the strong intermediate shooter as a trailer-shooter in the fast break system can be a devastating, almost indefensible weapon.

The objective in intermediate shooting should be somewhere in the mid-forties in percentage (slightly better than four made out of every ten attempts).

8. Free-Throw Shooting

a. The coach should select the style of free-throw shooting (underhand, chest shot, one hand, etc.) which is best adapted to the player's build, sense of judgment, and successful experience.

b. Free-throw practice should be

There is no fast break modification necessary for free-throw shooting. It might be pointed out, however, that the driving game of the cutters, in the outside lanes particularly, combined with their determination to score or be

Fundamental Skills to be Learned	*Fundamentals and the Fast Break: Modifications, Methods, Comments*

continued until the mechanics become "automatic." Thereafter, free throws should be attempted during "breaks" in the practice hour (when the player is fatigued).

fouled on the lay-up, nets these players more free throws than other players. The need for arduous practice for free-throw accuracy is therefore apparent.

c. Free-throw practice should involve competition between players as a means of attempting to stimulate some aspect of the game's conditions.

d. Spend spare moments on free-throw shooting. It will pay off!

e. Strive for *at least* 80 per cent accuracy under practice session conditions.

9. Rebounding

a. Improve jumping ability by leg strength activity and exercises such as:
1. Running cross country
2. Rope skipping
3. Leg weights
4. Leg exercises
5. Leg-use games

a. Cross country and rope skipping are highly recommended. Attached, low-weight leg weights for a limited running schedule is a productive method for increased leg power.

b. Set a jumping height objective and try each day to reach, equal, or surpass it. Set a new objective after working with techniques listed in "a." Jumping height objectives:
1. Touching the net.
2. Touching the backboard.
3. Touching the goal supports.
4. Touching the rim.

b. Select a height objective then practice jumping from the following positions:
1. Stationary — repeated jumps from a stationary position without shifting the feet as they contact the floor.
2. Jump and touch the objective with a one-step approach.

*Fundamental Skills
to be Learned*

*Fundamentals and the
Fast Break: Modifications,
Methods, Comments*

5. Touching a point above the rim on the backboard.

3. Rebound from a running start.
4. Fake left and/or right, then move in for rebounding position and jump.

c. With the ball, use the following skills for development of scoring by offensive rebounding:

1. Using full arm extension and jumping for height, two-hand rebound the ball against the backboard repeatedly. Fingertips only on the ball. ("Six times and in" is a good exercise.)
2. Same as 1, except use the left hand only on the left side of the backboard.
3. Same as 1 and 2, except use the right hand only on the right side of the backboard.
4. Alternate left and right hands on the left and right sides of the backboard.
5. Alternate left, right, and both hands on the left and right sides of the backboard.

c. With the ball, practice the fundamental rebound techniques as listed under "c," opposite side of the page.

1. Add: From the free throw line toss the ball high on the backboard, run in, rebound and control, tip the ball into the goal with:
   a. Both hands.
   b. Right and left hands on the left side of the backboard.
   c. Right and left hands on the right side of the backboard.
   d. Right, left, and both hands (on both sides).
2. Repeat "c1." using feints right and and left before moving in.

9

Drills for Fast Break Fundamentals

Drills for improving fundamental skills must incorporate speed of movement, quick change of direction, stopping, starting, pivoting, speed lay-up shooting, in-motion passing, and development of stamina.

Drill No. 1

Skills involved: Developing hook pass and baseball pass with each hand.

Directions: Pairs face each other, beginning at 6 feet separating to 50 feet, practicing the baseball pass and hook pass right and left handed.

Drill No. 2 (Diagram 117)

Skills involved: Dribbling with either hand, changing direction, pivoting, and reversing direction.

Directions: Line up players (or chairs) 10 feet apart; dribbler weaves in and out of line, changing hands or pivoting and reversing directions.

Drill No. 3

Skills involved: Ball handling, dribbling and shooting with speed.

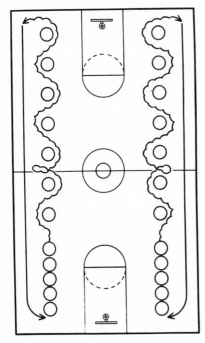

Diagram 117

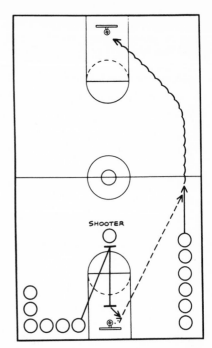

Diagram 118

Directions: Line up players into ones and twos. No. 1 dribbles ahead, stops, back pivots, passes to No. 2, who repeats the action. Continue court length and return. Watch footwork for traveling violation, stress clean passing and pivoting off either foot with left and right back pivots.

Drill No. 4

Skills involved: Two-man pass from back court for speed passing without violation.

Directions: Two lines of players opposite each other (8–10 feet apart) pass to each other down one side of the court, returning by opposite side.

Drill No. 5

Skills involved: Ability to pass to right and left with speed without violation.

Directions: Three lines with ball in center line starting pass to left or right for length of the court and return.

Drill No. 6

Skills involved: Handling the body.

Directions: Coach rolls ball across court or down court. Player races to the ball, picks it up, dribbles into fast lay-up. Several balls may be used for coach to roll after previous player starts drive.

Drill No. 7 (Diagram 118)

Skills involved: Long pass and drive by receiver.

Directions: One line of forwards and centers pass from backboard rebound to guards breaking from near center of court.

Drill No. 8 (Diagram 119)

Skills involved: Filling three lanes quickly.

Directions: Three players line up behind each other. Number 1 player dribbles straight down center. Number 2 player follows from the end line to mid-court then cuts to the outside lane of his choice. The third player fills the remaining lane. Pass-off is

Diagram 119   **Diagram 120**

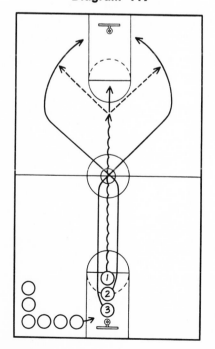

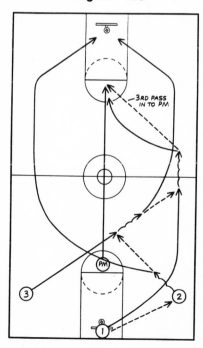

made by No. 1 at top of circle. Vary the position of the No. 2 and No. 3 players.

Drill No. 9

Skills involved: Passing, cutting, shooting.

Directions: Three-man weave or figure-eight drill with shooter varying lay-ups to include the Basic Seven. Passers vary direct pass with the bounce pass.

Drill No. 10

Same as Diagram 119 with pass back to middle man who shoots or passes to opposite cutter.

Drill No. 11

Same as Diagram 119 except cutter shoots over rim, banking ball for offensive rebound of opposite cutter.

Drill No. 12 (Diagram 120)

Skills involved: Speed shooting, passing, pivot man passing skill.

Directions: The pivot man is stationed in the center of the circle or in position at the high post to receive a pass from one of three cutters in the three-man weave. The fourth pass goes in to the pivot man, and the players continue their cut in the three lanes. Stress fast cuts, functional passing, and follow-up by the pivot man. After shooting, retrieve the ball and return, using the same drill to the opposite end of the court.

10

Team Drills for the
Fast Break Offense

Drill No. 1 (Diagram 121)

Skills involved: Rebounding, outlet pass, and filling the lane.

Directions: Several shooters shoot from 18–25 feet, corner-to-corner passing the ball from one to the other in order.

No. 2 players line up on end line and come out one at a time as far as the foul line to face shooter who is allowed to shoot. As the shot is taken, the facing player executes good rebounding footwork and techniques, retrieves the rebound.

A No. 3 player stationed in the middle of the court moves to a position along the side line for the pass, depending on

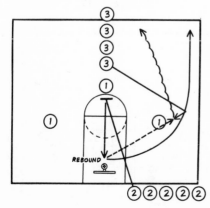

Diagram 121

which outlet pass is thrown. Right rebounds (from the shooter's viewpoint) are passed out to the right side line; left rebounds go to the left side lines; center rebounds go to the left side line, and shots which are made are quickly taken out-of-bounds and fired inbounds on the second or third step. After the pass-release, the passer follows as speedily as possible in the same lane to which he passed the ball. He stops at center in early drills; later, he goes the court length for lay-up shooting, taking the feed pass from the outlet-pass receiver, who has dribbled to the center lane and to the free-throw line.

Continuation: New players move to position for continuation of the exercise.

Drill No. 2 (Diagram 122)

Skills involved: Rebounding, outlet passing, filling the lane by two rebounders.

Directions: Same as Diagram 121 except two rebounders face the shooter; then, after rebounding, either rebounder takes the lane to which the pass is thrown; the remaining rebounder takes the opposite lane. The pass receiver dribbles the center lane, passing off to either cutter (rebounder).

Drill No. 3 (Diagram 123)

Skills involved: Rebounding, outlet passing, filling the lanes by two of three rebounders.

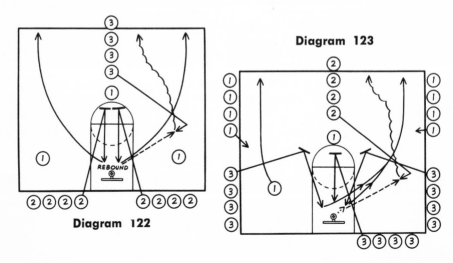

Diagram 123

Diagram 122

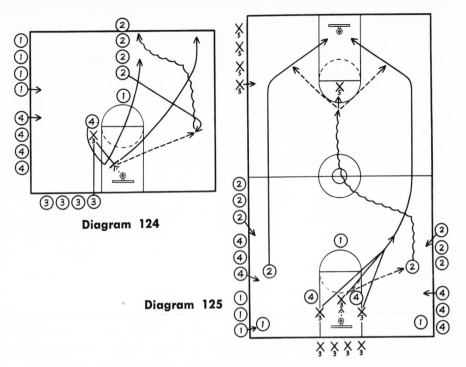

Diagram 124

Diagram 125

Directions: Same as Diagram 121, except three rebounders are used. The guard on the side line who does not receive the pass fills in his lane ahead of the ball. Rebounders sprint-race to the lane to which the ball was passed, the first one continuing on to the basket.

Drill No. 4 (Diagram 124)

Skills involved: Rebounding, passing, cutting, lay-up shooting, dribbling versus one defender. Also, offensive rebounding and fast break defense.

Directions: Same line-up as Diagram 123, except one offensive rebounder, 04, is stationed at the top of the circle. He (a) makes an effort for the offensive rebound; (b) tries to tie up the rebounder; (c) tries to block the outlet pass; (d) chases the cutters to stop the lay-up at the opposite end.

Continuation: This drill is repeated with two, then three, offensive rebounders.

Drill No. 5 (Diagram 125)

Skills involved: Same as Diagram 123 plus the skill of defending alone against the three-lane fast break.

Directions: Same as Diagram 123, except one defender is placed in the top of the circle at the opposite end of the court to stop the three men converging on the goal area. The three offensive rebounders continue working against the fast-break defensive rebounding and the outlet pass. They may chase the fast break players down court.

Continuation: Continue the previous drill using *two* defenders in the fast-break shooting area. All other factors in the drill remain the same.

Drill No. 6 (Diagram 126)

Skills involved: Same as Drills 1–5, Diagrams 121 through 125, except their execution is adjusted for free-throw play.

Directions: Repeat drills 1 through 5 (Diagrams 121 through 125) with one shooter shooting foul shots and the rebounders on the lane executing their defensive rebounding skills from these positions, passing out and filling the lanes, etc.

Additional drills: The coach's free-throw-made-and-missed, fast break plan may be practiced with the elements of these drills included.

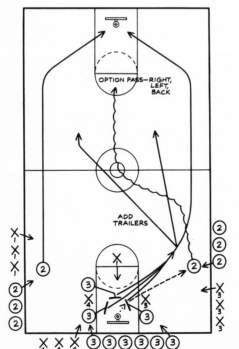

Diagram 126

See Chapter 6 for the "Trailer" drills designed for developing the trailer's ability to fill the lanes, his shooting, and his following up the offensive rebound.

See Chapter 7 for free-lance possibilities which can be made into drills involving three, four, or five players.

Also see Chapter 7 for coaching points from which single, double, and triple line drills can be devised.

Drill No. 7

Skills involved: Free lance involving 1-on-1 maneuvers.

Directions: Line up single-file facing as many goals as there are available. After instructions are reviewed, each No. 1 player in each line goes through maneuvers 1–15 (Chapter 7).

Continuation: Change positions of players.

Drill No. 8

Skills involved: Free lance involving 2-on-2 maneuvers.

Directions: Line up players in double lines facing as many goals as there are available. After designating Line 1 and Line 2 and explaining the responsibilities of each player, go through the 2-on-2 moves which will fit into your offense (Chapter 7).

Continuation: Change positions of players.

Drill No. 9

Skills involved: Free lance involving 3-on-3 maneuvers.

Directions: Line up players in three lines facing as many goals as there are available. After designating Line 1, 2, 3 and explaining the responsibility of each player, go through the 3-on-3 maneuvers which will fit into your offense (Chapter 7).

Drill No. 10

Skills involved: Free lance from the fast break which has been defended against by three defensive men.

Directions: Consult Chapter 7, devising drills to cover the free-lance maneuvers which are operated off the fast break.

Drill No. 11

Run these drills against one defender in the back court.

Drill No. 12

Run these drills against two defenders in the back court.

Drill No. 13

Run these drills against three back court defenders.

Part III

DEFENSE IN THE FAST BREAK

11

The Four Degrees of
Defense Theory

Players accomplish more in a learning situation when they are aware of the objectives involved. Players are stimulated further when they are given some idea of their position in relation to these outcomes. They learn better when they know where they are in relation to other competitors for the same position. Vague statements and generalized comments in answer to the questions on actual status are not appreciated nor are they fair. In a previous chapter, I emphasized the need and value of objectifying skills and performance for morale, for "psychological conditioning," for determination of personnel for various team assignments, and for the coach's need to be respected. In the theory of "four degrees of defense," there is drawn a definite line between one degree of defensive ability and another, in such a way that the degree of ability achieved will be clear to the player and his coach. Offense has long been measured. Practically every statistic written during a basketball game can assist in an offensive evaluation. By defining the defensive problems and observing how nearly the problems are realized, it is possible to assess objectively the defensive degree to which the player has advanced.

First-Degree Defense—Defensing (1) an assigned player. First-degree defense is applicable to those game situations which find one defensive man assigned to one offensive man (familiarly referred to as the "one-on-one" situation) who must be defensed when he is stationary or moving, with or without the ball. Some offensive maneuvers which are problems for the first-degree, defensive player are:

a. Defensing against the fake during and after passing the ball.
b. Defensing against the fake during and after the dribble.
c. Defensing movements prior to, and including receiving the ball.
d. Defensing faking which occurs before shooting.
e. Defensing the offensive moves after the shot (blocking the offensive follow-up).
f. Defensing the field goal attempt (the mid-air block).
g. Defensing the pivot man (a player who is in position to receive or does receive the ball with his back to the basket).

It is a fact that the first-degree defense (and less) characterizes the limit of most players' ability. To some extent, a demonstration of any degree of defense is influenced by the ability of the offensive player; however, and the proper defensive position, the proper application of sound countermechanics in the situation represent the factors which are used to judge the defender in his relationship to the first-degree goal. Can the player play the man assigned man-to-man (nose-to-nose) in the above situations? If so, he can play "First-Degree Defense."

Second-Degree Defense—Defensing (1) an assigned player plus (2) the ball. The ability of a defensive player to keep the optimum defensive advantage each time the ball moves requires *second-degree, defensive skill*. To be able to play the man assigned in relation to the ever changing ball position is required defensive play for this degree. The relative position of the defender in relation to the position of his man and in relation to the goal being defended is a fine adjustment natural to few. For most, it requires many tedious hours of practice. Examples of second degree situations are:

a. Adopting the proper position defensively when the ball is passed from one player (position) to another player (position). The essential skill is that of watching the man assigned *and* the ball and being able to play the ball and the man at all times, maintaining optimum position on each in relation to the scoring area.

b. Out-of-bounds plays—The difficult assignment of playing the man and the ball in situations where the ball is behind the defender is a real second-degree defensive problem.

c. Jump-ball situations—Each jump-ball circle requires the defense to assume a different position on the man and the ball. Each circle requires a defense involving playing the man and the ball.

d. Defensing the pivot man—Individual defensive play versus a stationary or moving pivot man must be of the second-degree level or the offense will take over completely. Here is a good example of an area of the game where it is impossible to defend a player (a pivot man) when you have no idea of where the ball is. It is also impossible to play the ball only and still keep a defensible position on the man. Second-degree defense is a must here.

e. Defense against the passer who passes into the pivot man is inadequate defense if both man and ball are not played simultaneously.

f. Rebounding—Defensive rebounding is best achieved when the defender plays the man first, then the ball. Some may try the reverse, but they fail because the players do not play both at the same time. Position play on the backboards is dependent on the second-degree defensive ability.

Players who can manage a second-degree performance are not

easily found. Coaching the awareness of and the skills necessary to rising to this level of defense is a worthy challenge for the coach and the player.

Third Degree Defense—Defensing (1) an assigned player, plus (2) the ball, plus (3) the offensive situation. That degree of defensive play in which the player recognizes and anticipates the offensive maneuver or technique being used, and by skill, ability and "know-how" eliminates the disadvantage to which he is being subjected. A third-degree defensive player must have these abilities:

a. Ability to slide through, slide under, or "over the top" of his teammates and their respective assigned players.
b. Ability to recognize or anticipate when and when not to slide.
c. Ability to switch.
d. The anticipatory knowledge of when to switch or when not to switch.
e. The cooperative technique involved in switching.
f. The ability to "beat the switch."
g. The individual and cooperative ability needed to defeat the "blind" screen, the stationary screen inside and outside, and the moving screen inside and outside.
h. The technique of beating the post play (when the pivot man is used as a stationary screen).

All good teams use various strategems involving two or more players to give the offense a temporary advantage. Inasmuch as there is already the advantage of prior knowledge on the offense's side, the problem of defeating the maneuver is almost insurmountable unless the defender is equipped with third-degree defensive ability. If he is continually caught in the offensive "traps," he is not in third-degree class. A player knows as well as the coach where he fits in this degree category.

Fourth-Degree Defense—Defensing (1) an assigned player, plus (2) the ball, plus (3) the situation, plus (4) helping a team-

mate with his assignment. The fourth-degree defensive player is quite rare. He represents the ultimate in defensive ability, and, given rebounding power along with this degree of skill, he is absolutely invaluable. The fourth-degree man not only covers the numerous assignments listed in the three previous degrees, he also assists his teammates with their individual assignments, and he does so in such a way that he sacrifices nothing in terms of carrying out his own defensive responsibilities.

The fourth-degree player is the "double-team" player, the man who helps "sandwich" the pivot man, the slough-off defender on the away-from-the-ball side of the court. He helps in defensive traps around the court, and he worries the man with the ball or the man about to receive a pass every time he is near him. He is the loose-ball recoverer, the jump-ball stealer, the "ball hawk." He can do his job well and help others do theirs. This is the type of player who makes a fast break offense move faster and more frequently. He is the player who makes defensive play a very important part in the *offensive* plan.

Objective measurement of defensive ability may not be completely feasible using the foregoing "degree" concept, yet it is certainly possible to categorize personnel with reasonable accuracy after applying this formula. The challenge implied is to improve the player's defense as a means of improving him as a well-rounded player. Good defensive play multiplies the opportunities for offensive action. Consequently, it enhances, rather than limits, the offensive-minded players and teams. The player who can add a "degree" or two of defense to his repertoire of skills will, without a doubt, improve his total game. The collective individual improvement will upgrade every phase of team play and add greater possibilities of consistent and rewarding performances.

12

Relating Defense to the
Fast Break Offense

The fast break offense is a full-court offense usually originating from the back court. The principal source of the launched attack is from the defensive rebound. Furthermore, for years this offense has been channelled from a zone alignment of some kind which waits for the rebound to be secured: No rebound, no fast break; no field goal attempts, no rebounds; no fast break, no offense. The "forcing" fast break cannot wait. The team must have more opportunities to score than those afforded by a missed field goal. A defense must be devised, developed, and applied which will multiply the scoring chances—one which complements the offensive idea.

All offenses should have a defensive idea which assists in making the offense more effective. Certain offenses are closely attached to the team defense employed. To couple a full-court, man-to-man, harassing, pressing defense with a slow, ball-control offense would be the height of incongruity. This exaggeration, however, should illustrate the point that offenses and defenses should indicate some degree of coordination and compatability.

Dr. W. F. Burghardt, whom I assisted in football at one time, successfully taught his linemen that the team *without* the ball was an *offense,* even though the opponents had possession, if

124

those opponents were back of the twenty-yard line. For years I have used this principle to correlate defense with offense. Even though the opponents have the ball in their possession, the team without the ball uses tactics to get possession which become part of the offense the moment the ball exchange occurs. In fact, some offensive move may be in the process of being made in anticipation of possession.

Some of the objectives of attack used by the defense may be listed as follows:

1. *Forcing the offense to mishandle the ball or to fumble the ball.* The defensive players should attack individually and double-team poor dribblers, poor passers, and poor receivers. They should be attacked:
   a. In the back court.
   b. As they near the ten-second line.
   c. As they cross the ten-second line.
   d. As they come to a stop after having crossed the ten-second line.
   e. In all corners of the front and back court.
   f. In all close-to-the-line areas.
   g. When isolated with the ball from their teammates.
   h. When their dribble is used up.
2. *Forcing passes which are interceptable.*
   a. Defensing players in such a way and in such positions as to make them throw the ball long and high.
   b. Overplaying the passer to force lateral passes.
   c. Separating the players to force the cross-court pass.
   d. Forcing the player into a back-pivot near the ten-second line so he passes blind.
   e. Pressuring the pivot man who receives the incoming pass.
   f. Pressuring the player who passes the ball in to the pivot man.
   g. Making the opponent speed up his game, including his passing game.

h. Changing the usual pass patterns to unfamiliar areas and positions.

3. *Trying for the jump ball situations.*
   a. With a double-team on an isolated back court man.
   b. Cornering a man (double-team a player in the corners of the front and back court).
   c. Quick attack on a "blind" dribbler (a player who looks at the ball when dribbling and who turns his back on part of the defense while dribbling across the court, down side lines, into the corner, along the base line, and down court after a back-court by-pass of his defense).
   d. Going after all loose balls.

4. *Forcing the opponent into a position from which the ball may be stolen.*
   Examples: 2b, 2c, 2d, 2h, 3a, 3b, 3c.

5. *Forcing a poor field goal attempt.* Every field goal attempt should be contested. Furthermore, the contesting should begin prior to the opponent getting to his shooting area and before he assumes shooting form.
   a. Do not allow the opponent to take his best or favorite shot. This not only refers to form but to speed also.
   b. Do not allow the opponent to take a shot from his favorite spot.
   c. Change his shot and his spot.

6. *Block the close, field-goal attempt.* A legal block of the close shot can be made by defensive men who have a good sense of timing, who can play the man and ball together, and who have good jumping ability. The idea here is to force even the close shot to be altered by the shooter, thus decreasing his percentage, increasing the possible defensive rebound possibilities.

In reiteration, let me state that any defense which is employed by a fast break team should originate and force those situations which increase possession and subsequent fast break thrusts. That defense, when applied, forces the offense to give up the ball.

Stating the theory of the complementing defense another way, the more quickly a defense can place offensive players (those who become offensive players on the ball exchange) in scoring position, the better defense for that offense it is. It is fairly obvious then that the defenses which are best adapted to realizing this objective are those which meet the offense in the back court, in, and close to, the scoring area itself. When there are interceptions, stolen balls, and loose balls which are retrieved in the back court area, there is little or no time for defensive adjustment. This inability of the defense to adjust is not confined to the players involved with the ball, neither can players without the ball adjust to those who are teamed with the defense. The pressure exerted by the offense to go forward against pressing tactics gives the advantage to the defensive team on the exchange of the ball. Before the adjustment can be made, the optimum scoring area is overloaded with offensive players. Diagram No. 127 shows the areas of the court where defense can give decided advantage to the team taking the

Diagram 127

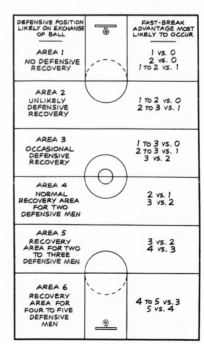

DEFENSIVE POSITION LIKELY ON EXCHANGE OF BALL		FAST-BREAK ADVANTAGE MOST LIKELY TO OCCUR
AREA 1 NO DEFENSIVE RECOVERY		1 VS. 0 2 VS. 0 1 TO 2 VS. 1
AREA 2 UNLIKELY DEFENSIVE RECOVERY		1 TO 2 VS. 0 2 TO 3 VS. 1
AREA 3 OCCASIONAL DEFENSIVE RECOVERY		1 TO 3 VS. 0 2 TO 3 VS. 1 3 VS. 2
AREA 4 NORMAL RECOVERY AREA FOR TWO DEFENSIVE MEN		2 VS. 1 3 VS. 2
AREA 5 RECOVERY AREA FOR TWO TO THREE DEFENSIVE MEN		3 VS. 2 4 VS. 3
AREA 6 RECOVERY AREA FOR FOUR TO FIVE DEFENSIVE MEN		4 TO 5 VS. 3 5 VS. 4

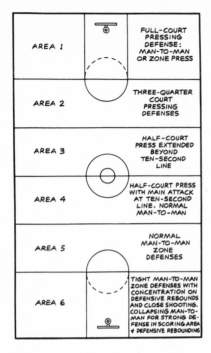

AREA 1		FULL-COURT PRESSING DEFENSE: MAN-TO-MAN OR ZONE PRESS
AREA 2		THREE-QUARTER COURT PRESSING DEFENSES
AREA 3		HALF-COURT PRESS EXTENDED BEYOND TEN-SECOND LINE
AREA 4		HALF-COURT PRESS WITH MAIN ATTACK AT TEN-SECOND LINE. NORMAL MAN-TO-MAN
AREA 5		NORMAL MAN-TO-MAN ZONE DEFENSES
AREA 6		TIGHT MAN-TO-MAN ZONE DEFENSES WITH CONCENTRATION ON DEFENSIVE REBOUNDS AND CLOSE SHOOTING. COLLAPSING MAN-TO-MAN FOR STRONG DEFENSE IN SCORING AREA & DEFENSIVE REBOUNDING

Diagram 128

ball from the offense. The diagram shows the offensive overload most likely to occur from various positions on the court when the aforementioned tactics are employed. It is obvious that the defenses most desired would be those designed to gain possession in areas 1, 2, and 3.

Following, is a list of defenses and their relationship to the offensive possibilities employed by a fast break team. These points are summarized in Diagram 128.

1. *Full-Court Press, Man-to-Man.* Defensive concentration is on areas 1, 2, 3 (see Diagram 128). It is primary, full-court defense and should be considered not only as a strategem but as basic to the development of effectiveness in other pressing defenses.

2. *Full-Court, Zone Press.* Defensive concentration is on areas 1, 2, 3. The advantage of the zone-press idea used with the fast break offense is in the automatic, or natural, alignment of players for an offensive advantage. The zone-press moves to a position of advantage in number with ease, since it is already in that position defensively.

3. *Three-quarter–Court Press.* Man-to-man and zone defen-

sive concentration is on areas 2 and 3. Ball possession in this area gives consistent advantage to offense.

4. *Half-Court Press.* Defensive concentration is on area 3 and the ten-second line area of area 4. The defenses which offer pressure at half-court are strong as a complementing defense for the fast break team. The advantage of such defense is as much with the team gaining possession as with others mentioned, except that the distance from the goal often allows for some defensive recovery. Therefore, defense in this area (3–4) requires that the third lane be filled on offense. The three-lane fast break becomes a necessary preparation, beginning with any defense applied to areas 4, 5, 6.

5. *Normal Man-to-Man.* The man-to-man defense is basic to all other defenses. A player who learns to play man-to-man defense can play any other defense more effectively. As a fast break complement, it has the disadvantage of a poor alignment of personnel for the three-lane idea. It is more difficult to teach the fast break from the man-to-man defense than from defenses with a zone principle. However, once the team learns to fill the lanes after having established certain responsibilities, it becomes a dangerous threat from areas 4, 5, 6.

6. *Pressing Man-to-Man.* This defense will do more to gain possession of the ball than the normal man-to-man defense because it is designed to keep pressure on the offense all over the front court. It also gives an advantage on the get away, that down-court, lead step which makes the fast break go. It is most effective in areas 4, 5, and 6, with particular pressure on the side line, corners, pivot area, and ten-second line territory.

7. *Zone Defense 2-1-2.* Defensive concentration is on areas 5 and 6. Omitting the defensive shortcomings of the 2-1-2 zone, it is the best formation for the fast break offense. It offers the best position for all assignments, including rebounding and filling the lanes with the desired players, using practically all variations. It offers a strong teaching basis for the assignments and responsibilities of the players and is very good for five-man practice drills. It requires a third lane for most of its success;

however, it is one of the best defenses to give a 2-on-1 situation from areas 4 and 5.

8. *Zone Defense 2-3.* Defense concentrates on area 6. This defense has most good points offensively shown by the 2-1-2 zone, with added strength at the boards.

9. *Zone Defense 3-2.* Defensive concentration is on areas 4 and 5. The 3-2 zone is very dangerous to any one- or two-out offense, since, when employed, it gives an immediate 3-on-2 fast break advantage from which the defense cannot recover. It offers the greatest automatic advantage from the area farthest from the goal and in an area where defensive recovery is usually otherwise possible. It suffers, however, in its inability to defense area 6 and in its two-man rebound responsibility.

10. *Zone Defense 1-3-1.* Defensive concentration is on areas 5 and 6. The main purpose of the 1-3-1 defense is not an offensive one. Other zone defenses could just as well be named zone offenses. The possibilities of using the 1-3-1 with the fast break are not as good as with other defenses. With emphasis on stopping the pivot man and the side-court shooter and being perfectly aligned for mass rebounding, the 1-3-1 is not readily adaptable to the fast break because its area of defensive concentration requires a fast break involving four to five players moving from the area of the best recovery (area 6) for the most defensive players.

11. *Other Zones.* Defensive concentration is usually on area 6. Although most added zones have some fast break opportunities to consider, their defensive value cannot usually give them a good offensive advantage.

12. *Combination Man-to-Man and Zone Defenses.* Defensive concentration is usually assigned. The value of combination defenses to fast break success is related to how much defensive pressure can be applied to the various areas. Naturally, the defense which uses double-teaming and triple-teaming tactics in areas 3, 4, and 5 will prove most helpful to fast break objectives.

13

A Defense to
Complement the Fast Break

There are numerous defenses devised to pressure the opponents. The previous chapter lists the various objectives of defensive attack. It is an accepted fact that the strongest defense for attacking purposes is the man-to-man defense. Varied zone defenses may be used, man-to-man defenses with a zone principle, zone defenses with a man-to-man principle, but, basically, the man-to-man factor is the essential ingredient in all pressure defenses. In other words, regardless of the defense used, that defense becomes a more potent weapon if the groundwork is in man-to-man fundamentals.

The "fast-breaking defense" is a combination man-to-man–zone defense, which I have used with small variation for a number of years. It defenses aggressively, harassingly, excitingly, frantically from end line to end line, with scoring from the defensive position as its principal purpose. Similar to the defensive platoon in football, the object is to create opportunities for scoring through the application of defensive power.

The prerequisite for a *fair* defense is first-degree defensive ability. Second-degree defense is needed for a *good* operation. Third- and, particularly, fourth-degree defensive strength virtually assures this *defense* to be one of the very best *offenses*

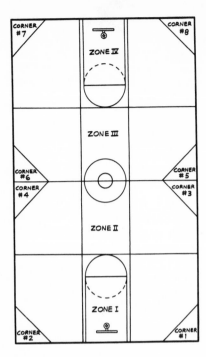

Diagram 129

available. Diagram 129 shows the court division for the administration of the defense, with four zones and eight "corners" indicated. The "corners" are the areas most vulnerable to defensive attack. The cornering defense simply uses the outside lines (and in corners 3, 4, 5, 6, the ten-second line) as an assisting agent in defensing the opponent. The zones are marked for purposes of strategy and understanding. Zone I extends from the back-court end line to the top of the back-court circle; Zone II extends from the top of the back-court circle to the mid-court line; Zone III extends from the center of the court to the top of the front-court circle; Zone IV extends from the top of the front-court to the end line. Diagram 130 illustrates the original defensive positions assumed by the players in the full-court press. These positions are assumed as quickly as possible by the team immediately after the following:

1. A field goal attempt, made or missed.
2. A free throw attempt, made or missed.
3. After a preplanned signal.
4. After a particular situation.
5. On the coach's instructions.

132

For purposes of clarity, the following discussion of assignments is made on the assumption that a field goal or free throw has been made. A quick-thinking defense can quickly transform a missed field goal or free throw situation into practically the same defensive application. The defense will be discussed by zones.

Zone I Defense

In situations where 01 takes the ball out-of-bounds at the end line, 02, the logical receiver for the first pass in-bounds, is double-teamed by X1 and X2. X1 takes a position in front of 02 or an overplay position; X2 is to the rear of 02 and blocks him from down court movement and forces 02 away from 01 and the ball. Both stay on 02 tight! They give their very best effort for at least three to four seconds, which is usually long enough to cause 03 to come to the ball, or move to a free space for the pass, or break to the ball close to the end line. 02 is blocked to the right side of the court if he gets the pass despite the opposition.

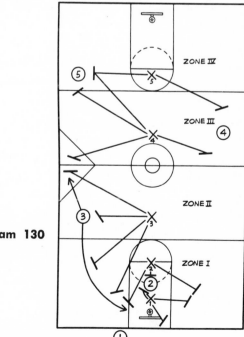

Diagram 130

If 02 moves to the end line or to the ball, X1 can assist in the pinch or switch to 01, with X2 now covering 02 alone. If 02 receives the ball, the play is to turn 02 into the side line away from 01, cornering him, if possible (in Corner No. 1), and forcing him to a stop. If X2 (in one plan) can force 02 to a stop, X2 *immediately switches back to a double-team on 01 or 03*, whoever is most likely to receive the pass (actually duplicating the original situation), Diagram 130, or he can force 02 to give up the ball in another plan.

Returning to the ball-out-of-bounds position, if 02 is covered so well that 01 is not likely to get the ball to him and 03 comes into Zone 1 for the first pass-in, X3 (who is the best defensive player) plays him straight man-to-man for all he is worth. In fact, X3 has played 03 straight man-to-man from the start. Should 03 get the ball, X3 turns him into the center toward X1 and X2 for double-team possibilities, or X3 turns him to the side line and/or corner (corner 4), forcing him to a stop. X1 overplays 01 now, and X2 keeps 02 man-to-man (Diagram 131).

Diagram 131	Diagram 132

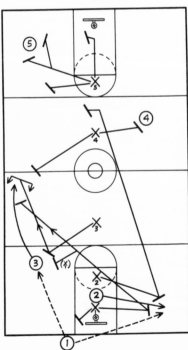 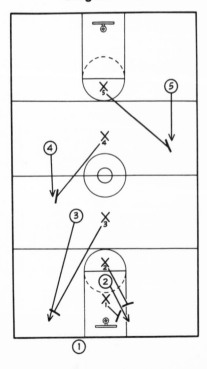

In offensive maneuvers in which one player goes behind the other for the pass back, the defense makes a quick, legal blocking-switch to the receiver, and at the same time, the defender switching to the passer blocks his move for any return pass. All players coming out of the back court should be obstructed or blocked from the down court pathways on which they have decided. This is a worrying, delaying, and often frustrating technique.

X4 and X5, during the defensive action in Zone I, play a zone-like position on 04 and 05 if they are down court in Zone III or Zone IV. They assume a man-to-man position if either 04 or 05 moves into Zone I or Zone II for the first pass-in (Diagram 131).

The defensive battle over Zone I is the defensive action which tells the story. It is actually a fight to maintain a sound position for five seconds! In some situations the element of surprise which is involved in the defense calling for one or the other plans of defense may account for one to two seconds. The defensive double-team on 02 could hold up the throw-in one more second. The look by 01 for 03 and the moving into position by 03 with X3 closing in may account for another second. There are 3-on-2 or 5-on-4 for four seconds! Then, look for the long pass to 04 or 05. X4 or X5, aware of the scene in front of them, must be prepared to pick this pass off! (Diagram 132)

Zone II Defense

Zone II is the second, big battleground. Once the ball is passed in-bounds there begins the new count of ten seconds. The defense has these few seconds to force the offense into an error. It has already been shown how a recovery in Zone I or II is hardly defensible. Any possession of the ball in this zone usually results in a score. The defense is an offense when it carries out its purpose.

Just as 03 must become a part of the offense when 01 and 02 are attacked by X1, X2, X3 in Zone I, 04 and 05 must enter the picture when the attack shifts in Zone II. The key to Zone II defense is the containing of 04 and 05. The objectives of such defense are therefore fourfold.

1. Keep the ball in Zone I and II, using tactics previously described.

2. Disallow the advance across Zone II by forcing the ball to a stop. Double-team the ball first, the nearest receiver next.

3. Intercept any pass which carries from Zone I to Zone III or Zone IV. X4 is the principal interceptor. X5 is the interceptor for Zone IV, but he must also serve as the cut-off man in the goal area of Zone IV to stop the drivers who may come in with the ball. The play for the interception must be sure, because failure here leaves the offense a free entry on the scorebook. X4 and X5, when not playing for the interception, play 04 and 05 with a loose, zone-like position, during which they play both the ball and their man.

4. X1, X2, X3 must interchange positions for defensive pressure possibilities on 01, 02, 03. (Diagram 133).

When the nearest receiver is away from the ball (cross-court) and deep down-court, X4 may leave his position to double-team 01, 02, or 03 if they appear about to escape by dribbling. X4 moves very quickly to block the dribbler. X2 who has chased 02 stays with him, running him into X4. X1 moves to the vacated area covered by X4 or to the offensive player who fills that area or rear area for the pass from 02 (Diagram 134).

The exchange by X1, for instance, or X3 for X5 may also occur, especially if there is no possible receiver in Zone IV or if there is no receiver moving into Zone IV fast enough to beat the exchange (Diagram 135).

The exchanges of X4 and X5 for X1, X2, or X3 are usually made with the idea of attacking the offense at the junction of the ten-second line and the side line or at the junction of Zones II and III (corners 3, 4, 5, 6). Passes from corners 5 and 6 must go in only two directions—laterally or forward. This trap, like all other corner traps (Diagram 129), relies on position, speed

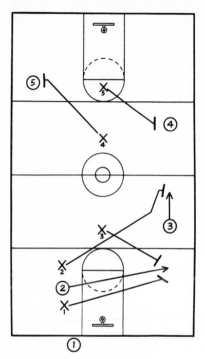

Diagram 133

Diagram 134

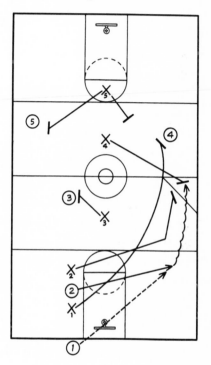

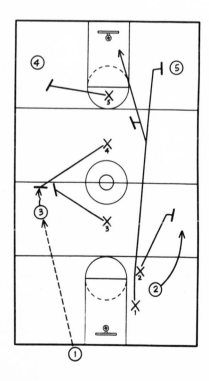

Diagram 135

137

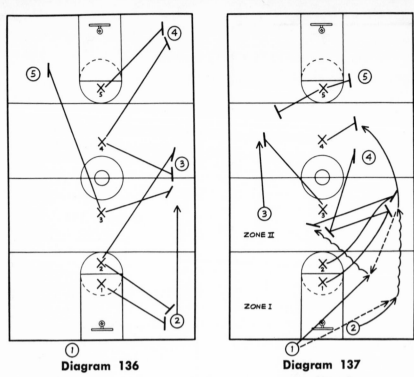

Diagram 136   Diagram 137

of attack, excessive up and down arm motion, but not toward the ball. (The offensive player moves the ball into your hands rather than your striking the ball out of his hands. Fewer fouls are called against the defense using this tactic than in the other.) Corner traps are shown in Diagram 136.

Players not involved in the double-teaming defense should:

1. Look for the pass toward the goal.

2. Look for the pass to the receiver moving into position for the player's relief.

3. Look for the forced, high loft pass to any receiver.

4. Anticipate interception and possession.

5. Be poised for the fast break!

An earlier trap is set when the defense forces the ball to the side line and then moves in front of the player and close into him with hands high. This forces the pass up into the air for a possible defensive recovery. Such traps occur in any zone but are more effective in Zones I and II because of the ten-second time factor, which is, of course, a psychological agent working for the defense.

In the event an offensive player, for example 02, advances up

138

court to Zone II and is confronted by the defense and passes back to a fellow player in Zone I, the defense on 02 may shift to the receiver and double-team him, leaving X4 to defense the passer (Diagram 137).

X1's Defensive Back-Court Play. Other techniques involved in the "Fast-breaking Defense" are those involving the number-one point or chaser, player, X1, who has the following responsibilities (Diagram 138):

1. He defenses the player who is the main receiver for the first pass-in.

2. He may switch to the player passing the ball in-bounds.

3. He chases the ball and the receiver anywhere in back-court Zone I and Zone II.

4. He makes the exchange in defensive assignments by assuming the responsibilities of the players moving into position for blocks, traps, and cutoffs.

5. If he is behind the ball, he sprints for a double-team, or he temporarily moves into the back court for assistance to X4 or X5 in stopping possible penetration by the offense.

X2's Defensive Back-Court Play. (Diagram 139).

Diagram 138   **Diagram 139**

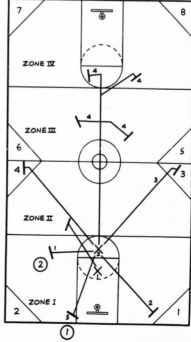

1. X2 defenses player 02, who is the main receiver for the first pass-in.

2. X2 is assigned to stay with 02 whenever he goes in Zone I and Zone II.

3. X2 is responsible for the defensive mechanics which force 02 to the side line or into corners 1, 2, 3, 4, 5, or 6. Where other assigned players assist in taking the ball, he forces the interceptable pass or a tie-up. In forcing a player to the side line, the defense takes a moving position alongside and slightly to the rear of the dribbler. This position makes the dribbler go in the direction the defense wishes him to go. The defense must not allow the dribbler to change direction and go inside or to his rear with the change of hand or go-behind-the-back dribble. He gradually forces the offense to the side line or corner, boxing him in "against the side lines." The defense has the problem of keeping the dribbler from outspeeding him or moving out ahead of him. If this happens, the defender must discontinue following the dribbler in a circle and straight line it across the arc and meet the dribbler as he comes out of the curve—Head him off at the pass.

4. X2 makes a move deep into Zone III or Zone IV to recover from 02's possible escape, helping with defensive play en route and recovering and picking up 02 again when advisable.

5. X2 should strive for interchangeability with X1.

X3's Defensive Back-Court Play. X3 has one of the most important defensive assignments and may need to be the strongest 1-on-1 defensive player on the team. (Diagram 140).

1. X3 defenses 03 man-to-man all over the back court. 03 is usually the main player effecting a release from back-court, pressing defenses.

2. X3 does all he can to force 03 to the side line or corner trap 3 and 5 or 4 and 6. He does this by allowing him dribbling action in the direction of the trap, but not enough advantage to beat him.

3. X3 may exchange with X4 or X5 on defensive play which

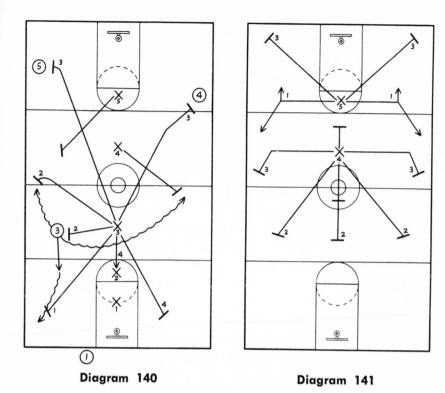

Diagram 140   **Diagram 141**

has X4 or X5 blocking the sideline drive of 03. This move usually occurs after the double-team attempt.

4. X3 should be able to carry out the assignments of X1 and X2.

X4 and X5's Defensive Back-Court Play. The back-court play of X4 and X5 is limited. It is a factor only when 04 and/or 05 may be employed in the back court offense. In such instances, X4 and X5 leave their zone positions and go into a strict man-to-man defense to cut off any pass-in to their assigned players. (Diagram 141)

Zone III Defense

Zone III represents the area of defense previously described as that beginning at mid-court and extending to the top of the circle in the front court.

Pressure applied in Zone III is a continuation of the pressure begun in Zone I and Zone II. Pressure is most effective just at the moment the player crosses the ten-second line. Unless the

141

offensive plan against the press takes the ball all the way to the goal or deep into Zone IV, the defense has a valuable ally in the brief feeling of relaxation which takes place as the offense escapes from the back court. (Some teams actually stop their press-escape offense with the pass or dribble that barely clears them across the ten-second line.) The aggressive pressure is continued, and action is renewed and tactics from the half-court press are incorporated into the defensive plan. Blocking the pathway of the passer or dribbler, overplaying the possible deep receivers, forcing the dribbler to the side line and corners (corners 5 and 6), and pushing the offense out against the ten-second line are other half-court, pressing measures. (Certain half-court pressures are also exerted in Zone II, especially on the back-court side of the mid-line.)

Zone III is the last line of defense from which the fast break offensive is launched with minimum preventive possibilities. (Diagram 142)

Zone IV Defense

Although the pressing defense, as it is thought of, occurs in Zones I, II, and III, there is some pressuring possible in Zone IV. However, for fast break purposes, the Zone IV defense allows only the kind of fast break attack which operates against the normal defense thrown against any team which secures the ball. Corners 7 and 8 are important in the "fast-breaking defense" in instances of the long passes from the back court to 04 and 05. X4 and X5 force the receiver in these corners. It is most difficult to pass from this and under pressure without the ball going to the defense. A fast break offense from Zone IV takes the form of the fast break as regularly operated, except in the aforementioned examples. Pressure applied to players in the Zone IV area may create in the offense an element of uncertainty, which is helpful to the fast break success of the defensive team. It realizes one of the most important objectives of defense, that of multiplying offensive opportunities. (Diagram 143).

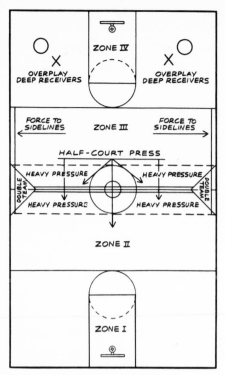

Diagram 142

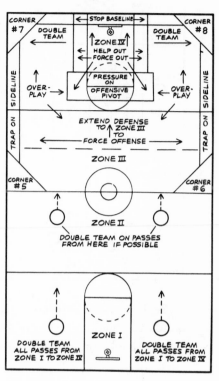

Diagram 143

During pressure in Zone III, X4 and X5 have the primary responsibility of cutting off any move toward the basket by a dribbler or receiver. Their secondary responsibility, however, is to play for the interception, overplaying 04 and/or 05. A third task in Zone IV for either X4 or X5 (whichever is assigned) is that of defensing the offensive pivot man, who is one of the main relays for cutters breaking out of the back court. In Zone IV these players play a normal defensive position but must do so with gusto.

Important points in the "fast-breaking defense" are:

1. The highest degree of success of this pressing defense is based on knowledge and execution of the fourth-degree, defensive skills of the players on the team. It can be successful to a great extent without all players being so endowed.

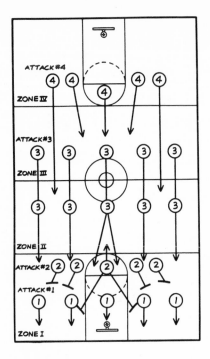

Diagram 144

2. The main defensive attack can be divided into several kinds of attack to be applied on signals given by "the defensive quarterback" or on instructions by the coach: (Diagram 144)

Attack No. 1—The defense uses straight, man-to-man defense on all offensive players, beginning at the end line and forcing them to unfavorable positions by single-player aggressiveness and ability or double-teaming.

Attack No. 2—The defense does not press the player passing the ball inbounds but, rather, begins the attack by double-teaming the player who is to receive the inbounds pass.

Attack No. 3—All defensive players withdraw to Zone II, III, and IV. The second the ball is passed inbounds, the attackers pick up their preassigned men in Zone I.

Attack No. 4—All defensive players withdraw to Zone III and IV until the first pass-in is made, then the attack is made in Zone II with the pick up by preassignment.

3. Various numbers, names, words, or situations may be employed, or other signals may be devised to indicate the type of attack which is to be made. All defensive positions are assigned in relation to the offense and in relation to the zones

144

and are immediately assumed on signal, according to previous plan.

4. The defense fast breaks to their assigned, preliminary positions, then to their assignment. This fast movement to position is especially necessary for players X3, X4, and X5. X1 and X2 are usually in a ready position with a little adjustment.

5. Use the man-to-man, half-court press when all of the offensive players are in the process of moving to Zone III and Zone IV or go to a normal position defense, man-to-man or zone, with pressing tactics incorporated. For instance, when one offensive player is strongly attacked in the front court or on the side line, or in corner 7 or 8, each player within range of the pass immediately plays in front of his man (overplay). Interceptions from any overplay position give an instant, fast break advantage.

Teaching the "Fast-Breaking Defense"

Listed below are the progressive steps in teaching the defense under study (defensive players strive for interception, forced violation, or tie-up): (see Diagram 129).

1. 01 passes inbounds to 02 versus X1 from behind the end line, using the Zone I area only.

2. 01 to 02 versus X1 and X2 in Zone I only.

3. 01 to 02 versus X1 and X2 in Zones I and II combined.

4. 01 passes inbounds from end line to 03 in Zone II only.

5. 01 passes to 02 and 03 versus X1, X2, X3 in Zones I and II combined.

6. 01 passes to 03 versus X3 in Zones II and III combined.

7. 01 passes to 04 versus X4 in Zone II only.

8. 01 passes to 04 versus X4 in Zone III only.

9. 01 passes to 04 versus X4 in Zones II and III combined.

10. 01 passes to 03 and 04 versus X3 and X4 in Zone II.

11. 01 passes to 03 and 04 versus X3 and X4 in Zones II and III combined.

12. 01 passes to 02, 03, 04 versus X1, X2, X3, X4 in Zones I, II, and III combined.

13. 01 passes to 05 versus X5 in Zone III only.

14. 01 passes to 05 versus X5 in Zone IV only.

15. 01 passes to 05 versus X5 in Zones III and IV combined.

16. 01 passes to 04 and 05 versus X4 and X5 in Zone III.

17. 01 passes to 04 and 05 versus X4 and X5 in Zones III and IV combined.

18. 01 passes to 03, 04, 05 versus X3, X4, X5 in Zones II and III combined.

19. 01 passes to 03, 04, 05 versus X3, X4, X5 in Zones II, III, and IV combined.

20. 01 passes to 02, 03, 04, 05 versus X2, X3, X4, X5 in Zones I, II, III, and IV combined.

21. 01 passes to 02, 03, 04, 05 versus X1, X2, X3, X4, X5 in Zones I, II, III, and IV combined.

Interchange all positions offensively and defensively for best results.

14

Fundamentals and Drills
for the Defense

A. FUNDAMENTALS

Defense is important to basketball success. Contrary to general opinion, the fast break relies to a great extent on defense, although it is the only offense which can manage victories on occasions with poor defense or a glaring lack of it by abandoning all but a semblance of defense and concentrating on scoring only. Admittedly, the dependence on such strategy is second best to strong defensive play.

Strong defensive play by individuals is determined by the degree to which a player realizes the following objectives of defense (in sequence, from greatest to least difficulty):

1. The defense must keep the offensive man to whom he is assigned from receiving or otherwise gaining possession of the ball.
2. When the offensive player has possession of the ball, the defense must not allow him to advance it by dribbling or passing.
3. The offensive player must not be allowed to pass the ball to the point of his choice. He must be forced to pass elsewhere.
4. The teammate of the offensive player must not be allowed

to receive the ball in the position of his choice. He must be forced out of position.

5. The defense must not allow the offensive player to shoot the shot he wants from the spot he wants. Force the shooter to a spot of secondary choice.

6. Neither the offensive player nor his teammates must get a second shot. No offensive rebounding allowed!

Various team defenses are based on one or more of the above objectives and the methods used to achieve each. The best team defenses are built on good individual defensive ability. The following fundamentals are essential to the development of individual defense:

Defensive Stance—the Basic Defensive Position

The player should adopt a comfortable stride-stance position with the weight equally distributed on both feet, legs semi-flexed, head level, eyes ahead, right arm raised above shoulder-level. If the right leg is forward, the left arm is down and slightly out from the body. The arm positions are reversed if the left leg is forward.

The feet-parallel position must be used for lateral defensive movement, but it is less effective than the stride position.

Defensive Sliding

The player must learn to move forward, backward, left and right, circling left, circling right, keeping proper balance, moving with a "boxer's shuffle." For those players whose best stance has the left foot forward, advance the left foot when moving forward, then quickly move the right or rear foot the same distance. Use the reverse technique when the right foot is forward. When moving right, move the right foot first, bringing the left foot along the same distance the right foot is moved. When moving left, reverse the above technique. Never cross the legs during the sliding motion. Never bring the feet together but rather keep them apart (shoulder width) with an equal weight distribution over each.

Defensive Running

A different type of defense must replace sliding when the opponent moves with speed. Down-court or vertical movement by an opponent requires a defense involving in-step movement, herein referred to as "defensive running." To practice mastery of this fundamental, a player may work on the following techniques:

1. Run forward four to five short, fast steps; stop; keep balance.
2. Follow (1) by running backward; stop; keep balance. (When running "backward," run forward looking backward by rotating the trunk instead of backing straight back.)
3. Run right; stop; keep balance; change direction.
4. Run left; stop; keep balance; change direction.
5. Combine 1, 2, 3, and 4.
6. Keep the body flexed with the center of gravity low.

Defensive Rebounding

Fundamentals	*Fast Break:* *Modifications and Comments*

Defensive rebounding can be improved by attention to the foregoing skills mentioned under "Rebounding 9a and b" (Chapter 8). Others can be practiced as follows:

1. Blocking-out exercise—Use a quick reverse of position, from facing the offensive opponent to one of facing the goal, and almost simultaneously move laterally left and right, gauging the ball's

The defensive rebound is the beginning point of the greater percentage of fast breaks; consequently, there should be a considerable amount of time spent on perfecting the art and modifying it for fast break purposes.

Inasmuch as the objective in defensive rebounding is to retrieve *and* pass the ball out away from the goal to a teammate, the emphasis is placed on these *two* points instead of the *one* of

Fundamentals

Fast Break:
Modifications and Comments

possible rebound; move in toward the backboard and, with a high, leg-spreading jump, secure the rebound.

This technique calls for the rebounder to be in motion toward the backboard rather than rebounding from a static position.

2. The one-hand reach for the ball enables the rebounder to secure the rebound inches higher. Such rebounding is permissible if the ball is guided to the opposite hand (in a lower plane) but is still kept high and away from the body. Elbows are flexed slightly outward and the ball is extended even farther away from the body as the feet contact the floor.

3. A sure, effective, rebounding technique is accomplished with a two-hand, overhead grasp and a noticeable flexion of the trunk (jackknife action), with legs extended outward during the jump but adducted to shoulder width on contact with the floor. A pivot step away from the opponent toward the base-line will give added protection against the attempt to tie up the ball at this point.

4. Hold the ball tightly with a

simply getting the rebound.

The faster the pass-out or outlet pass, the better. Several points to be considered in training for the fast break rebounds are:

1. Rebounding and a quick release.

2. Anticipate the target's (player to receive the pass) position prior to and while gaining the rebound.

3. Practice moving after a jump on contact with the floor from a square stance to a stride-stance with a half-turn from the waist, so the ball can be protected as the player looks downcourt prior to the pass-out. If the rebounder plans to pass out to his right, he turns the ball so his right hand is behind the ball ready for the baseball-type pass. A slight variation in body position readies him for the one-hand, bounce pass, the overhead, two-hand pass, or the hook pass, all working well against possible contest.

4. The defensive rebounder follows his pass by moving down court into one of the open lanes.

To summarize:

The fast break offense requires

Fundamentals	*Fast Break:* *Modifications and Comments*
strong grip. Practice holding the ball against one or more players trying to take it away.	a rebounder to be responsible for four very important tasks:
5. Use the defensive, blockout technique explained in 1 at different distances from the goal.	a. Secure the defensive rebound. b. Throw the outlet pass. c. Fill the open lane. d. Follow-up rebounding on the offensive boards.
6. Practice rebounding *next* to a player as well as from in front of him.	
7. A team is only as good as its rebounding. Individual rebounding skill improves team or group rebounding.	

After the foregoing offensive skills have been thoroughly learned, a player is ready to apply them against an opponent.

B. DRILLS

Aside from the drills and coaching points just mentioned, the following drills are some of those I use to develop individual and team defensive skills. All of these drills involve the entire length of the court.

Drill 1. (Diagram 145)

Skills involved: Defensive sliding and defensive footwork.

Directions: Players are divided into two stationary lines with five to six players eight to ten feet apart. Another line of players is on defense opposite still another line of offensive players. The first offensive player in line runs slowly between the stationary lines, weaving in, out, and around the stationary players, as his defensive player matches his offensive movements.

In the first exercise the players hold their hands behind their backs to develop leg power.

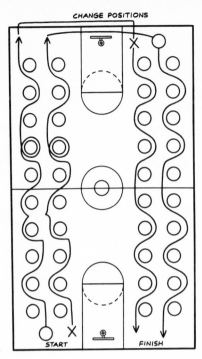

Diagram 145

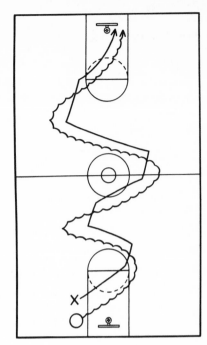

Diagram 146

In the second exercise the players on defense use their normal defensive posture.

Continuation: In subsequent exercises, the offensive players may speed up their movements. Reverse the drills so as to develop the ability to move both right and left.

Drill 2. (Diagram 146)

Skills involved: Defensing the dribbler.

Directions: Starting at the end line, the dribbler moves the court length as the defender, with hands held behind him, uses his footwork to keep good position to block the dribbler's pathway and force him to change direction.

Continuation: Use same drill, using normal defensive position for attempted steal, tie-up, or force to a stop.

Drill 3. (Diagram 147)

Skills involved: Two men defensing the dribbler.

Directions: One defender waits at the foul line, another at mid-court. The dribbler begins from the end line. Both defenders attack to take the ball, tie up the dribbler, or force him to a stop, all without fouling. If the ball is taken, the players go for the basket.

Drill 4. (Diagram 148)

Skills involved: Changing direction during retreating defense or changing the foot which is forward.

Directions: One player on offense, one player on defense. The offensive player runs in angles the court length, using only half the court width; the defensive player stays within six feet, matching every move without using arms (folded behind). Change positions and return on the opposite half of the court.

Continuation: Same, using normal defensive action.

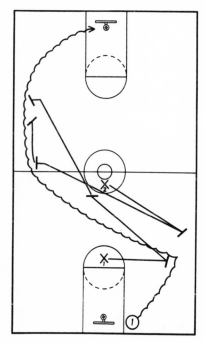

Diagram 147

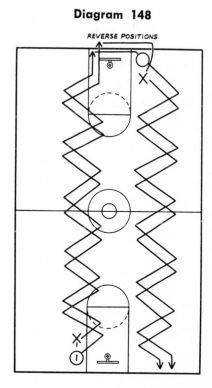

Diagram 148

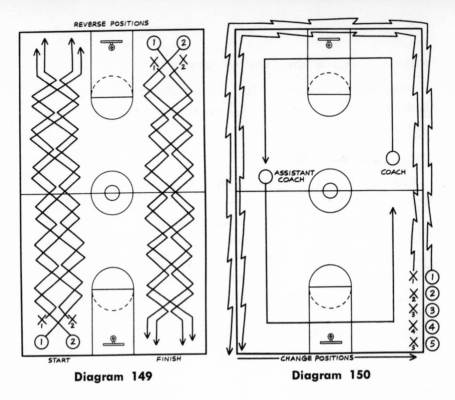

Diagram 149　　　　**Diagram 150**

Drill 5. (Diagram 149)

Skills involved: Switching while in motion backward.

Directions: Two players on offense zigzag run down-court, using only half the court width. Two on defense stay within six feet of the others, switching at each crossing of the offense. Keep hands clasped behind as in first exercise.

Continuation: Use normal defensive action.

Drill 6. (Diagram 150)

Skills involved: Fundamentals of defensive movement.

Directions: Line up players at corner of court, one line outside of court, one line inside. The outside player is on offense; the inside man is on defense. The offensive player runs forward, stops, starts, runs back, slows down, speeds up, etc., all around the outside of the court; the inside player defenses every move of the offensive player. The next two players may follow when the first two have a half-court start. Use this drill first with hands clasped behind the back; then, in normal defensive position.

154

Continuation: Reverse the action, start from the opposite corner.

Drill 7. (Diagram 151)

Skills involved: Defensive cooperation between two players.
Directions: Two on offense with the ball attempt to go the length of the court against two defensive players.

Drill 8. (Diagram 152)

Skills involved: Cooperative defense, including double-teaming.
Directions: Two players attempt to take the ball the length of the court against three players who double-team one player. If the ball is taken from the two offensive men, the defenders fast break for the lay-up shot.
Continuation:
    a. Three players versus three
    b. Four defensive players versus three
    c. Four defensive players versus four
    d. Five defensive players versus four

Diagram 151   **Diagram 152**

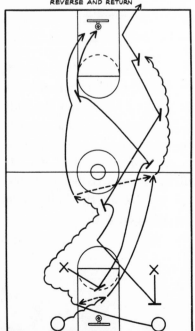
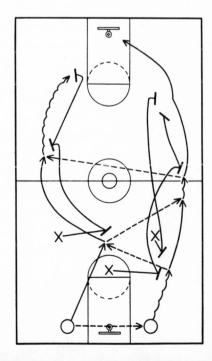

Drill 9. (Diagram 153)

Skills involved: The press, double-teaming, and fast break.

Directions: Three players, the first in each of three lines, with the middle man dribbling the center lane versus two on defense. The two defenders, in breaking-up the 3-on-2, try to get

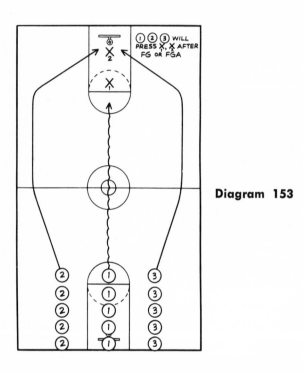

Diagram 153

across the ten-second line if they get the ball in their possession. The three players on offense, after scoring, or if the ball is taken from them by interception, defense, or rebound, become a pressing team of three, taking the ball before the two original defenders can get across the ten-second line with it and scoring again and again until the escape is made by the defense. Afterwards, three new players bring the ball down until the entire line has tried to score against the two on defense.

Part IV

CONDITIONING FOR THE FAST BREAK

15

Physical Conditioning for the Fast Break Offense

In the fast break offense, the physical condition of the player is especially important. If Team A and Team B are equal in every way except that Team A is using the fast break offense, Team A has the advantage. Team A must be in better physical condition for its offense than Team B must be for its system of play. Physical condition, as important as it is to all systems of play, is more important to the fast break game.

The ultimate conditioning program is one, by the attitudes and actions and leadership of the players, which would have the players living within a set of strong training rules throughout their athletic careers. This does not simply mean during the practice and playing season, but in and out of season for the entire high school and/or college participation period. The collective practice of the rules of healthful living offers a strong foundation for a rigorous conditioning program and finds participating players better equipped for the total practice-playing schedule.

Educate the Player

Education of the players in relation to the values of year-round training is the first step in the physical conditioning of the fast break team. Education is superior to enforcement if for no other reason than the fact that the coach is unable to enforce training rules after the school year ends. Education yields cooperation beyond requirement; enforcement yields acquiescence within the rules only. I might say, at this point, that if the players are not aware of the values of the training rules and their tremendous importance to the conditioning program, whatever form that program may take, the conditioning program will fall considerably short of its goal. Short of the best possible training program, which would be in effect at all times, but best in probability of acceptance, is the school-year training period. "The athlete will observe all training rules during the school year."

Finally, the in-season training period, although still the most widely accepted and practiced, is the least effective training plan when compared to the school-year plan and the all-year plan. As widely practiced as it is, the in-season training period is gradually losing ground. The better teams around the country and, indeed, the better individual performers, in my observation, are those whose *training programs are lengthened* by understanding and appreciation of the values of constant adherence to healthful practices, whose *conditioning programs are augmented* by participation in additional sports programs or schedules of fitness activity, and whose *practice periods are increased by off-season productiveness* through individual initiative and conscientious application. Great players and great teams always do more than they are required to do.

Training Systems

The foregoing remarks on the training program are intended to illustrate the need for a basic position from which to condition a team. Any conditioning program which is not undergirded by a strong training program is impractical or at least lacking in potential effectiveness. Realizing the need for superior condition as a prerequisite for successfully employing the fast break offense, I employ cross-country running. As a boxing coach in earlier coaching years, my teams went through my three-year tenure without sustaining a single knockout. Road-work, as well as skill, was a deciding factor in their ruggedness. It transferred easily to basketball as a means of readying a team for competition.

Personal subscription to an idea, however, does not mean it is necessarily acceptable to others. Many coaches, and many more players, do not agree with the cross-country roadwork method of conditioning a basketball squad. There are other good ways of doing the job. If the coach and players have un-limited time, for instance, three hours practice time or more per day, the cross-country program added to such an extended period would probably do more harm than good. Among the added values, other than total body exercise sustained and sup-ported by distance and time to force the body into its physio-logical conditioning processes, the cross-country program cuts down on practice hours spent in the gymnasium. Weight-training programs, isometrics programs, rope-skipping, and calisthenics can be adapted to do likewise. However, I am in-terested in a system which requires little or no equipment and which is challenging to a player in terms of his learning so that he will become personally responsible for his own con-ditioning progress. I feel any conditioning program must have as an incentive, or as a recommendation for its use, the possi-bility of readily observable results, of readily comparable re-sults (for competitive purposes), and the adaptability to the "honor" system operation. Cross-country roadwork meets these criteria.

Sixty-Minute Plan

In a number of instances the player wishes to condition him-self, both prepractice and off-season, with a program combining vigorous exercise, skills, and drills. To these conscientious and anxious-to-improve basketeers, I recommend the "60-minute self-improvement plan." Very often, I include directly under the title on the direction sheet, these words: "Guaranteed, with daily use, to improve any player." Wherever possible, the following should be preceded by coaching in the technique being practiced.

BASKETBALL

60-Minute Self-Improvement Plan

"Guaranteed, with daily use, to improve any player"

Item	Minutes	Activity	Description
1	5	Dribbling	Dribble in correct form forward, backward, stop, start, change hands, etc.
2	5	Passing	Use all types of passes correctly against wall with bounce-to-floor return, if alone, or to each other in dual situation.
3	5	Altman Jumps	Jump and touch rim, backboard, or strings, depending on height. Jump repeatedly 6 times without shifting weight on contact with floor. Rest 10–15 seconds, repeat, rest, repeat, etc.
4	10	Rebound Control A. Two-hand rebound B. Left-hand rebound C. Right-hand rebound D. Alternate (left-, right-, two-hand)	For 2 to 3 minutes each, rebound the ball against the backboard, using each of four techniques (see listing opposite). Rebound at full extension and maximum jumping height.

Item	Minutes	Activity	Description
5	5	Defensive Slides	Assume correct defensive stance. Slide forward, backward, left, right. Use 3-step slide and stop, change direction.
6	5	Lay-up Shots	Shoot 50 shots in 5 minutes using drive from top of foul circle, recover, shoot, recover, etc. Lay-up shots from right, left, down-center, cross-over, cross-under, and others.
7	5	Defensive Runs	Assume correct defensive stance, run 5 steps, stop, change, run forward, backward, left, right.
8	5	Intermediate Shooting	Shoot 25 shots in 5 minutes. Shoot 15–21 feet out. Follow shot before it touches floor, return to shooting area, shoot, follow, return, etc.
9	5	Rockhurst Special	From the free-throw line, run and jump high to touch backboard on alternate right and left side of the rim, run back to foul line, run, touch backboard, then back to foul. Continue at high speed for at least 12 trips in one minute, rest 10 seconds, continue.
10	10	Court-length Sprints	Sprint the court length at top speed, walk across the end line at moderate speed, sprint the court length, etc.

60 Minutes

I recommend the foregoing plan as a squad or team conditioner. It is adapted to group action. Items 3, 5, 7, 9, 10 form an abbreviated "30-minute conditioner" which requires no equipment. As has been mentioned, many carry-over skills are involved.

Player Cooperation

Regardless of the merits and demerits of one system or another, it is a fact that no system of conditioning is successful without the cooperation of the players in the matter of training rules. Under various coaching conditions with players of all ages and experience, my first effort is toward educating the player to the following facts:

1. That maximum personal achievement cannot be reached if certain rules of health are broken.
2. That the team suffers if each player is not doing the best job of which he is physically capable.
3. That teammates, team fans, and the public cannot have confidence in a team on which there are players who break the rules.
4. That the coaching staff loses confidence in such players also.
5. That even the least-skilled player can condition himself as well as the best-skilled player.

In high school and college situations, I always try to encourage the idea that, "once you sign up for the varsity, you are in training for four years, in season and off." This is the ultimate idea coaches like to see enacted by their charges. So far, my in-season rules are required; my off-season rules, which are the same, with the exception of diet regulation, are strongly urged but have no punitive action attached. The list is brief, but required, and enforced.

1. No alcoholic beverage of any kind.
2. No smoking or use of tobacco in any form.
3. No late hours—11:30 p.m. lights out rule except under conditions rating a prior excuse.
4. Diet on all trips strictly regulated by the coach. At all

other times, "use your own discretion in accordance with proper diet for athletes in training."

5. *Open Rule:* "Any action which limits your ability to give your maximum effort in competition should be eliminated."

The degree to which education replaces the need for enforcement indicates the degree to which a team is improving its collective conditioning, and, in many cases, it is also an indication of team unity and spirit. Forceful and impressive in the training philosophy and practice, especially with lower age groups such as junior and senior high school boys, is the self-imposition by the coach of the same rules which he asks his players to observe.

Cross-Country

Cross-country roadwork can be regulated to prepare a team for practice, for the playing season, for special occasions (such as post-season tournaments) to bring a team's general condition back to "peak," and occasionally as a disciplinary measure. I have used it for all purposes.

The cross-country program for basketball players can be incorporated into the regular school cross-country program if the cross-country coach is agreeable or if he can afford the time to include them. The objectives set in his program are usually sufficient to assist the player toward his conditioning goal. The good thing about the regular cross-country personnel operating the program is that the player is being conditioned prior to the opening of the basketball practice season. When the practice season does begin, the player is ready for rigorous work. In those situations where the basketball, cross-country program cannot be worked into the regular, school cross-country program, the basketball team student-helpers can easily manage the task. A good feature of cross-country running is the fact that little equipment is needed. The open road and a timepiece will suffice. One timer with a record book completes the administrative force.

Setting the number of cross-country miles to be run and specifying the time in which the distance is to be negotiated prior to the opening practice date has the following advantages:

1. Presenting the objective to the player in advance gives him an idea of the goal toward which he is working. He runs with added purpose.

2. Competitive course timings are stimulating and challenging; interest is maintained.

3. The miles to be run assist in eliminating those candidates who are not serious about training and also those who are not very serious about competing for membership on the basketball squad. It eliminates those who are unsure about the "price" they will have to pay for making the team, thereby leaving a group of dedicated candidates for the season's program. A rigid roadwork requirement "cuts" the squad.

4. The cross-country program allows the coach to use his practice hours for basketball skills and techniques rather than to use his valuable time for conditioning drills which are often unrelated to the system.

"63 Championship Miles"

My three-time National Champions (National Association of Intercollegiate Athletics) of 1957, 1958, and 1959, who won 95 out of 102 games for Tennessee A & I State University, always preceded the season with "63 championship miles," which meant 3 miles per day for 21 consecutive days immediately prior to the opening date. Only those 3 miles counted which were run in 20 minutes or less. I have no doubt that this method of conditioning contributed significantly to the success of this great team. For either the high school or college program, I would suggest that conditioning begin not less than three weeks before basketball practice starts. Of course, the length of the practice season before the playing season begins will have some effect on the length of preseason conditioning. The same schedule applicable to prepractice build-up may be used before the season's opener.

Some additional factors to be considered before posting the distance-time schedule are these:

a. The age of the candidates.

b. Their general physical condition (physician's report).

c. The length of time before the first game (overtrained athletes go "stale").

d. Weather conditions. Have a substitute conditioner for inclement weather.

e. The class schedule. Check to see if it will allow for running within the school day.

f. The after-school hours schedule, such as the study hour, the work hours, the recreational hours, etc., in which the students participate.

g. A consideration of their attitude toward the value of the method.

h. Modify your cross-country time and distance requirements if your team is composed of boys of high school age.

i. Consider other adjustments which may be necessary.

Other Training Plans

Although it is my conviction that cross-country running is the best answer to conditioning a basketball player totally, there are several good methods which might be used as alternate plans where cross country is not practical or where a coach or player wishes to exercise choice. I would say rope-skipping is the next best method. Except for the equipment needed, the attention to timing, and the skill necessary to make it beneficial, I would rank rope-skipping (boxers' style) number-one as a total means to body-conditioning. As a bad weather, indoor method it is a good substitute for cross-country. Furthermore, rope-skipping is very good for improving the coordination and footwork of the boy who is above-average in size.

Another very good alternative to cross-country is field ball, a vigorous, outdoor, action game, which is excellent for building stamina. Official, men's volleyball ranks third on my list although the exercise value may be somewhat limited by the skill of the players. For specific body-building, isometrics and weight-training are advised. Indoor training may consist simply of court-length sprints (described in the "60-Minute Self-Improvement Plan") for a period not less than 10 minutes—a very strong conditioner.

Reference has been made to cross-country running on the "honor system." When a team finds a cross-country program is helpful to its improvement, the "honor system" is easily installed. Under other conditions, depending, of course, on personnel, the system may be used. "Honor system" simply means the player runs the course, timing himself and reporting his time to the team manager or coach or posting it on the bulletin board in the team locker room. He has written his cross-country schedule into his daily class schedule. Before, between, or after classes, early morning, lunch hour, after class, or in the evening, he runs the course on his honor. Aside from being a great time-saver for the timers, who do not now have to be on the scene, this plan makes conditioning become a matter of individual responsibility and achievement, a very important factor in team morale development. If the player-coach relationship is not strong or if the squad or any squad members cannot be trusted, this method should be forgotten. It is only for "special" players and teams.

Three-Week Program

Following, is a suggested three-week, cross-country conditioning schedule for basketball players:

First Week	Running Schedule	Time and Distance
Day 1, 2, 3	High school and college: Alternate half-speed running and normal walking. Speed up each from day to day.	220 yds. for each (running and walking) for one mile to one mile and a half. No time limit.
Day 4, 5, 6	High school and college: Eliminate walking, speed up running day by day.	Time, at Day 6: H.S.—½ mi., 2 min. 45 sec. Col.—½ mi., 2 min. 30 sec. H.S. and Col. outside limit, 3 min.

Second Week

Day 1, 2, 3	High school and college: Alternate quarter-mile runs with 100-yard walks.	10 to 15 minutes of work.
Day 4, 5	Alternate half-mile runs with 200-yard walks.	15 to 20 minutes of work.
Day 6	Run 1, slow mile	H.S.—6 min. 15 sec. Col.—6 min.

Third Week

Day 1, 2	Run 1, slow mile	H.S.—6 min. 15 sec. Col.—6 min.
Day 3	Run 1 mile	H.S.—6 min. Col.—under 6 min.
Day 4	Run 1½ miles	H.S.—10 min. Col.—9 min.
Day 5	Run 1½ miles	H.S.—9 min. 30 sec. Col.—9 min.
Day 6	High School: Run 1½ miles College: Run 2 miles Alternate: 1 mile	H.S.—9 min. Col.—12 min. Less than 5 mi.

The above schedule has been worked out over a period of years. It has been applied to many age groups and is minimal in its demands. The times are minimum and designed for squads, not individuals. At the same time, the schedule will bring strong conditioning to a team in a relatively short period of time.

After three weeks of cross-country, if the playing season is as far away as two to three weeks, I suggest the "Third Week, 6th day" schedule be re-run two to three times per week, with the player advised to fill in with more work if he needs to do so and to be excused on off days if he is running well (without undue physical distress).

During the playing season, if the games are frequent, your cross-country program should have done the job with a final condition status in mind. However, if there are signs of deteriorating physical condition appearing in practice or game, individuals or the squad should be reassigned to roadwork to "bring them up again." An added value associated with the cross-country plan, in my experience, is that there are few players who will "break training" under the insistence of the roadwork, time-distance requirements. This roadwork program was applied to my squad of post-college, AAU players (Cleveland Pipers). They immediately returned to their college-training habits in order to make the squad physically stronger and more durable. The pay-off was the National AAU Championship in a league where all players are practically equal, but where individual and team physical condition is the telling difference between the champion and the challengers.

This conditioning factor is often the case in other leagues, in other settings. My most recent team, Kentucky State College, managed its best season in 13 years with the fast break "machine" operating on roadwork-conditioned "cylinders." I recommend it highly.

16

Psychological Conditioning
for the Fast Break

The fast break can be identified as an offense based on the *simplest* mechanics but requiring the *most* in determination. It is a game where the application of psychology to aid the player's belief in the game is necessary. Following, are some of my ideas on individuals and teams in relation to psychological conditioning.

Psychology is a science, a study of the phenomena of the human mind. Few avenues for its application are more open than those found in the area of competitive athletics. Consequently, regardless of whether or not there is any technical or academic basis for assuming the role, the coach finds himself in the position of applying psychological principles to many varied situations.

In all circumstances human behavior requires directed response; competitive athletics are no exception and demand a knowledge of cause and effect, of action, reaction, and interaction. Competitive athletics exaggerate the response. The test of the participants, coach, player, and spectator comes in their learning to direct these responses, to direct the energy associated with heightened enthusiasm and increased determination into channels which will bring favorable results.

In order to be instrumental, the coach, who is the key figure in this experience, must acquaint himself thoroughly with the background, experience, attitudes, habits, and ambitions of each of his charges. In this manner he may come reasonably close to prescribing proper types of stimuli and to predicting the possible response of each individual and the group to competitive conditions.

It is a fact that psychology applied to one player may be worthless when applied to another. It is difficult to find any one formula for a team which will inspire all members equally. Certain occasions, particular rivalries, and traditional contests may leave little need for the coach to "get his team up" for the game, but there are numerous contests when the team requires some kind of lift.

Aim at the Championship

One form of motivation which has a lasting effect is the one wherein the coach and players have a long-time objective, one which covers the entire season. The State Championship, the Conference Championship, or the National Championship as the long-range, constant objective requires little reminding and offers a goal which is renewed each time the team gets together. I believe next in importance are objectives which serve as means to the end, since to realize the immediate is a prerequisite to the ultimate. As an example, let me give the goals which I have always set for my college teams:

1. Win the National Championship

This is the long-range, ever-present, distant but achievable objective. It is always before us and influences our every act.

2. Win the Conference Championship

A closer goal, but one on which candidacy for the National Championship depends. It has often been the greater satisfaction for some players; however, it is a stepping stone to the big championship.

3. Win the Home Games

The objective here is immediate. This is a large and inspiring achievement involving local prestige and honor. It is a worthy goal. Defending the home court should be one thing which requires less stimulation than other situations. In fact, there may be a need to ease up on the home game pep talks since tension and feeling may surge too high for a sound game.

4. Point for the Away Games

The games away are the key games in the campaign. Careful attention to overconfidence or underconfidence must be given. Overcoming restricting effects of strange territory and its differences in courts, officials, food, fans, and other factors requires constant gauging of individual and team attitudes and reactions.

Use Statistics

As far as the fast break is concerned, there are certain psychological conditionings which seem to be applicable. The strenuous aspects of the fast break game call for other incentives. Added to those general attitudes which are discussed hereafter, it is often helpful to present statistics which demonstrate the necessity for constant effort in the running game. Reference is made here to the "Fast Break" column which indicates how often a player participates in a necessary aspect of the system. Placing this and other factors on a competitive basis according to positions has considerable value.

Game objectives, aside from specific strategy regarding specific opponents, are continually reiterated, reminding the players of their individual and team responsibilities and urging them to "give everything" by playing *their* game "all the way." Outrun them! "Out board" them! Be tireless! These are reflections of the team's intentions and the coach may further stimulate the individual team members according to his estimate of their receptiveness.

Physical Condition Necessary

I have said earlier that it is my belief, derived from observation and experience, that there must be a strong underlying program of physical conditioning for individuals and teams who plan to surpass others. Psychology applied to persons attempting to function efficiently without good physical conditioning brings negligible results. Inspiration, a form of psychological stimulus, may serve to carry competitors beyond the normal physical limit on occasions, but it should never be depended upon. It certainly cannot produce consistency in performance.

In the fast break offense wherein psychology is to be used as a force determining consistent, outstanding performance, the subject must possess well-conditioned physical equipment. The very knowledge of its possession places the individual or team in a favorable psychological position. There is a readiness for the application of attitude-influencing ideas which will produce and sustain the desired interest in and effort toward achievement.

Physical and psychological conditioning, then, are interdependent. Considering good physical condition as a state of readiness from which to begin participation in competitive situations is essential to the proper psychological conditioning of the player. *Physical conditioning is not an objective in athletics, it is a prerequisite.* Working industriously and diligently to arrive at peak condition merely sets the stage for development of our ultimate objective. From this point only the individual or team is capable of reacting effectively to the application of certain applied psychological stimuli. For instance, one of my theories is that "fatigue is purely a psychological phenomena," that an individual with the desire to win ignores the very thought of fatigue as long as he is in the position of realizing success. The very idea of fatigue cannot occur to him under such circumstances.

I have often used this example to "prove" to young players that fatigue is psychological and not physical at all. "If a player should run a couple of miles and at the end of this distance fall completely exhausted on the ground, energy too dissipated to move another inch, then, if out of the nearby woods should come a ravenous lion approaching the prostrate, would-be victim, why is it that this lion's bait will get up and run a mile or more to safety, completely oblivious to his supposed exhaustion? It is simply that there happens to be a goal so great (that of saving his skin) that fatigue becomes completely unimportant. The goal of winning can be so powerful and so demanding that fatigue becomes a negligible or forgotten matter."

Two Important Factors

Coaches should know more about the factors of psychological importance which determine sustained interest and application of effort in competitive athletic participation. They are the objectives pursued by those who want consistent, seasonal and year-to-year performance by athletic teams. Outlined here are some of the psychological factors which are of utmost concern to all involved in competitive athletics:

1. *The aims of the coach and team must be mutual.* They must be clear to both and both must work together in their efforts to realize a common aim.

2. There must be set forth *an aim which is greater than winning,* but which carries winning with it. Winning should be considered not as a goal in itself but rather as something incorporated in the goal. Substitute goals, such as "striving for excellence in performance" or "trying for a creditable team effort," are objectives which have a more permanent appeal. Winning games in the *process* of attempting to reach a greater goal is a more worthwhile and meaningful experience than winning as an *end* in itself.

Reaching the team and its individual members through psychological motivation techniques in respect to this "substitute" goal may prove less monotonous and more challenging. The intelligent athlete often tires of the old, morale-raising clichés. To be sure, during game competition there is always the immediate goal of trying to best the adversary. Team members should be made to realize, however, that their intent in securing this immediate goal is actually a phase of a larger plan. This does not eliminate but, rather, emphasizes the gathering of all available skills and strategy in answer to the task of the moment. The most reliable estimate of individuals or teams cannot be made except by observing and judging them in the highly competitive situation. The response to the emergency at hand, however, is only part of the progressive experience of the persons involved.

The goal of "striving for excellence in performance" is a realistic one, attainable only through persistence. The interest in a goal of this nature should increase through one contest after another. It does not diminish after the less permanent and comparatively easily achievable goal of winning a game has been met. Continuing interest results when the objective is stimulating and within possibility, but difficult to reach. It is thus possible to reach the goal while losing or to lose the goal when winning.

Evaluate the Team's Performance

Parallel to this principle is the fact that interest in reaching an ideal is more easily maintained if the participant knows his position in relation to his goals at all times. There must be some means by which the team and its members may determine their individual and collective positions in relation to the objective. This calls for a periodic evaluation of the individual, with findings translated into subjective and objective terms. Subjective rating of players, while not highly reliable, still represents the coach's opinion. This is a strong force in the behavior and attitude of the player. The player's struggle for the coach's approval is the basis of the directing and coaching influence.

The factors which I use on a 1 to 10 rating scale are listed below in Chart I. By adding the column ratings across, an individual's rating is determined. Ratings are made according to position; that is, guards are rated with guards, forwards with forwards, etc. Adding the columns down and averaging the total gives the coach an idea of the team's approach to a 10-point rating in each area. Motivation for team improvement is based on down-column averages.

Game Statistics

The interpretation of game statistics is the basis for our objective evaluation method (see Chart II). During practice sessions, two days of the week are devoted to game-condition scrimmages during which a battery of trained student statisticians chart eighteen different factors in game performance. These statistics are summarized and reviewed according to team position; that is, guards are charted with guards, forwards with forwards, and centers with centers. A listing of the factors which can be measured, evaluated, and interpreted, and which can figure in an objective rating of players according to their position is shown in Chart II.

In the chart, five guards are rated against each other. Check the small number in the upper right-hand corner of each columnized factor. In column FGM, for instance, 8 FGM by Hunter is ranked No. 1, the 6 FGM by Adams is second (see 2 in the upper right-hand corner), Russell with 4 FGM is third, Miller with 3 is fourth, Barnhill with 2 is fifth. Each factor is ranked similarly; the ranking numbers are then added. The player with the smallest total receives the highest rating. He comes closer to first place on the average than any of his competitors and is thus the better all-around performer in the game

Date: 2/4/70 Game: TIGERS vs. INDIANS Score - We ___ They ___ Game factors to be rated	Player	HURLEY	FOX, R.	WALTERS	EVANS	NELSON	HUGHES	HOLMES	LEE, L.	THOMAS	ROCHE	CRAWFORD	WILLIAMS	HENRY	Team average in skill rated
Maximum - 10 pts. Average - 6 pts.	No.	2	3	4	5	33	34	35	40	41	42	43	44	45	
Minimum - 1 pt.	Pos	G	G	G	G	F	F	F	F	F	C	C	C	C	
General Skills, Speed, Movement		6	8	7	9	9	8	7	6	7	8	8	9	6	7.5
Individual Offensive Skills		7	7	7	6	7	7	6	5	8	8	8	9	6	7.0
Team Offense: Responsibilities, Execution		7	7	7	7	6	6	6	6	7	7	7	7	7	6.7
Individual Defensive Skills		8	8	8	8	8	7	7	7	7	8	8	8	7	7.6
Team Defense: Responsibilities, Execution		6	6	6	8	6	6	6	7	6	6	7	8	6	6.5
Fast Break: Responsibilities, Execution		7	8	9	7	8	9	7	8	9	9	8	7	7	7.9
Rebounding (Centers & Forwards) Aggressiveness (Guards)		8	8	8	8	7	7	7	7	8	8	8	9	7	7.7
Practice Performance		8	8	8	9	8	8	7	7	8	8	8	9	7	7.9
Morale, Attitude		10	10	10	9	9	9	9	9	9	9	9	10	10	9.4
Physical Condition; Stamina & Endurance		7	7	6	6	5	5	5	6	5	7	8	9	9	6.5
Points		74	77	76	77	73	72	67	68	74	78	79	85	72	
Rank by Position		4	1	3	1	2	3	5	4	1	3	2	1	4	

The heading spanning the top: Individual and Team Basketball Rating System

Chart 1

Date: 1/31/70 Game: PIRATES vs. THOROBREDS	Player	HUNTER	RUSSELL	MILLER	BARNHILL	ADAMS	BROWN, F.	BARNETT	BROWN, J.	JONES, S.	PEERMAN	ROBERSON	SATTERWHITE	WARLICK	WARLEY	Total
No.		3	4	5	6	7	22	23	33	34	35	44	45	46	47	
Pos.		G	G	G	G	G	F	F	F	F	F	C	C	C	C	
Field Goals Attempted		16	12	9	3	18	8	7	6	4	8	12	12	14	6	135
Field Goals Made		8 [1]	4 [3]	3 [4]	2 [5]	6 [2]	4	5	2	1	5	8	6	4	4	62
Field Goal %		.50 [2]	.33 [3]	.33 [3]	.67 [1]	.33 [3]	.50	.71	.33	.25	.63	.67	.50	.29	.67	.46
Free Throws Attempted		2	2	1	1	1	4	5	1	1	4	2	2	0	2	28
Free Throws Made		1 [1]	1 [1]	1 [1]	1 [1]	0 [5]	2	4	0	0	3	1	1	0	0	15
Free Throw %		.50 [3]	.50 [3]	1.00	1.00	.00 [5]	.50	.80	.00	.00	.75	.50	.50	–	.00	.54
Total Points Scored		17 [1]	9 [3]	7 [4]	5 [5]	12 [2]	10	14	4	2	13	17	13	8	8	139
Shooting Index		400 [1]	133 [3]	99 [5]	133 [3]	198 [2]	200	355	67	25	315	536	300	116	268	3145
Personal Fouls		4 [5]	2 [2]	3 [4]	1 [1]	2 [2]	4	2	5	5	3	4	4	3	4	46
Offensive Rebounds		0 [4]	0 [4]	1 [3]	3 [1]	2 [2]	2	2	3	0	3	3	4	4	5	32
Defensive Rebounds		2 [3]	2 [3]	1 [5]	4 [1]	3 [2]	6	6	6	2	6	7	8	9	6	68
Total Rebounds		2 [3]	2 [3]	2 [3]	7 [1]	5 [2]	8	8	9	2	9	10	12	13	11	100
Assists		5 [1]	3 [3]	3 [3]	5 [1]	3 [3]	2	2	1	0	3	4	6	5	3	45
Recoveries		2 [5]	3 [3]	4 [2]	5 [1]	3 [3]	1	1	0	0	1	2	1	1	0	24
Held Ball: Defense		2 [1]	0 [3]	0 [3]	2 [1]	0 [3]	1	2	1	0	3	2	2	1	0	16
Fast Breaks		6 [2]	2 [5]	3 [3]	7 [1]	3 [3]	2	5	2	3	4	3	2	3	5	50
Degree of Defense		4 [1]	2 [4]	3 [3]	4 [1]	1 [5]	1	1	1	1	1	2	2	3	1	2
Miscellaneous																
Miscellaneous																
Time Played		30	35	10	15	35	30	40	10	10	35	30	20	35	20	
Rating		34	46	47	25	44										
Rank		2	4	5	1	3										

Score - We _____ They _____

Individual and Team Basketball Rating System

Chart II

which has been charted. Cumulative ratings will give a longer look at the individual. Seasonal ratings can also be based on a master sheet of cumulative statistics in each factor.

These records are posted weekly for each candidate, also cumulatively for the entire squad. Both subjective and objective ratings are posted throughout the season. Actual game performances are charted and the resultant ratings are influential in the selection of players who are to dress for the game, start the game, or make the trip. Finally, the ratings serve as an important factor in awarding the varsity letter. Indiscriminate rating or evaluation of players, where they are all listed together (perhaps alphabetically), regardless of their positions and functions and responsibilities, makes statistics a useless expenditure of time and energy. It is indisputably "good psychology" to be able to discuss with a considerable degree of objectivity the relative merits of individuals according to their positions. Each player knows the statistical formula for his rating. He also knows the skills which must be demonstrated and made a part of playing performance. Providing the climate for improvement and interpreting effort and performance in a way which can be understood gives the coach a solid background for positive appraisal—a good basis for honest psychological stimulation.

Other Procedures

Other procedures which have definite psychological possibilities are recommended as follows:

1. Keep players psychologically pliable by being honest and fair in all dealings with them.

The coach must maintain the confidence of the players. Unless he can do this, there is no way he can possibly exert the kind of influence over them they will need in their development. He must act in such a way that there is a mutual feeling of respect for each other. Players play their hardest games for a coach whom they trust and admire because of his impartiality and fairness. The "inspired" games are never born in an atmosphere of distrust.

2. *Make practices short, active, enjoyable, and instructive. Do not use meaningless drills.*

Practice sessions lasting beyond the point of interest lose much of their value. Learning takes place more surely when the practice schedule is active and challenging and the drills have a clear relationship to the systems of offense and defense. In my own situation, practices last no longer than one hour and a half and follow a more instructive line since the player conditions himself on his own time. There is an effort to keep the practice from the extremes of either labor or frivolity and to make them more businesslike and continuously fast moving.

3. *Set up hypothetical ratings which you feel should be standards for individual and team progress.*

Earlier in the chapter, the objective rating plan is explained. As a psychological move to stimulate team progress, the team average may be set for any factor on the rating scale. Effort can be made by individuals to improve their previous marks in designated areas in actual games and in scrimmages. Increasing team rebounding offensively and defensively, increasing field goal percentage, decreasing the loss of the ball, decreasing fouls, and increasing free-throw percentages are all associated with team improvement.

For individual motivation, friendly competition by positions in certain statistical areas (excepting field goals) is advised as a means toward better over-all performance. The standards set should be within range of the individual or team. There is always room for continued improvement in basketball.

4. *Use interesting, meaningful motivation methods for individuals and team.*

Special recognition by the coach for those phases of the game which are generally overlooked is good for team morale and motivates improved play. Awards and certificates for the player with the best free-throw percentage or record, the most assists, the best field-goal percentage, the fewest turnovers, the least fouls per game, the most offensive rebounds, and so forth, are all good incentive-builders. In addition, published statistics among the athletic family or in the local newspaper in regard to the above factors may also serve as a real motivation to team members.

I recall that with the Cleveland Pipers, 1961 NIBL Champions, to offset too much concern over individual high scoring, we agreed to count rebounds as points among the highly competitive centers and forwards. When a player came out of the game with 14 points and 6 rebounds, his actual score as far as the Pipers were concerned was a 20-point night. Many times, our players who were lacking in high-scoring ability gained the most points of the evening by going after the rebounds. The Pipers were in the league two years and led each of those years in offensive rebounds, partly as a result of rebound emphasis being used to motivate special effort in that phase of the game.

To improve the free-throw shooting of one college team I coached, a large, glass bank was kept in the teamroom into which the player who missed free throws in the game would have to pay a dime for each free throw missed. The bank filled up, and it was great fun, but I discontinued the practice after collecting a sizeable sum. The players became so nervous about paying out dimes they missed more often than they did before we started the idea.

Of course, competitiveness, whether against others or against a standard, forms a basis for comparison. As long as the intensity of personal feelings is kept down, and as long as it does not engender bitterness or ill feeling, it is a good practice. A good competitor thrives on competition. The coach can always use this very strong drive in his program.

5. *Attempt to create an atmosphere of confidence for the player to grow in.*

One of the surest ways to gain confidence is to achieve. The player who learns to do one thing very well is often quite self-confident and has also won the confidence of others.

Do not set goals for a player which are beyond his ability. This may set the stage for frustration and the lack of confidence which goes with failure. Spend time and patience on the player so that he can contribute to the game. Show approval of all sincere effort. Add to the strength of the player by being helpful, attentive, interested. Counteract critical remarks and evaluations by others. Keep the player striving but set realistic stages of progress which he can discern and which will bolster his morale as he moves along. In general, be encouraging and be careful with caustic remarks, sarcasm, and criticisms made in emotional situations. Be firm but be friendly.

6. *Help the player to feel that the system of play is not too difficult for his ability.*

The success of any system is largely dependent on the belief of the players in their ability to make it pay off in terms of its objectives. When they have this feeling and the feeling that each can individually carry out his assignment and do a good job at it, team morale becomes a positive, observable attribute.

Keeping the system simple is helpful. The fundamentals may be difficult enough. Why add to a player's problems by complicating the offensive and defensive assignments? The better your players, the simpler you keep the system. Do not nullify above-average ability by making the system complex. Players enjoy playing in a system in which their particular good points are emphasized rather than detracted from. They appreciate carrying out assignments in which they can excel. As long as the coach makes them feel there is a place in the system for them, they also appreciate having to compete with others for the privilege of making the team.

The late Dr. James Naismith, inventor of basketball, once said: "Basketball is a game many can play but few can master." In this statement lies the challenge of both physical and psychological conditioning in athletics—mastery of the game. In response to this challenge, the coach must devise means by which each individual player and the team, of which he is a component, can visualize the myriad requirements in fundamentals, techniques, and skills necessary for such mastery. Then, through his methods, his spirit of determination, his zeal for achievement, he can imbue his players with the need for continuous and conscientious application. A team member must practice and play with *mastery of the game* as a general objective and with the mastery of a specific assignment as his part in the fast break offense.

Part V

CONCLUSION

17

Fast Break,
Championship Style

There are almost as many ways to play basketball as there are coaches to coach the game. However, various systems of offense and defense have been devised by individuals in the profession who have attempted to express, through team action, some game philosophy, some set of principles, or some group of objectives. The fast break offense is an example of one of these systems. In each instance, the performances by individuals who adhere to these objectives and by coaches who direct them serve to emphasize the strength and weaknesses of the system employed. The fast break has been tried, tested, and found true. Many coaches and players have made their contribution to this type of game by developing its tremendous number of skills and techniques. My version of the fast break is simply the result of trying to keep the good, eliminating the ineffective, and staying with those practices which make the system most likely to succeed regardless of the defenses applied against it.

Coaches and players alike are marked by the type of play which brings them attention and success. Opponents seeking to overcome that coach devise many tests for his system; some are orthodox, some unorthodox, some sound, some outright gambles. Each attack brings an answering adjustment which solidifies the system, strengthens it, makes it adjustable and flexible to the degree that it can remain a known weapon in the coach's arsenal. This is what has happened in my own experience. I am sure it has happened to many others in theirs.

Basketball is everchanging. No one offense is versatile enough to withstand without adjustment the onslaught of the multiple defenses and defensive variations employed by teams today. Yet, no offense should be so fundamentally weak that it must be completely abandoned or made unrecognizable at the first sign of a change in defensive tactics. The principles of offensive play should maintain their identity regardless of the situations met. The fast break system used by my teams over the years has the same objective it has always had. The mechanics change to meet various defenses, and some ways of executing a particular skill have been adjusted to keep the fast break moving; certain techniques have a flexibility about them which allows game-by-game changes and within-the-game variations, but the original intent of the fast break offense still requires more men on offense in the close-to-the-goal, high-percentage, scoring area than there are defensive men in the same area.

In looking at the entire idea of the fast break offense, I am positive that part of its soundness as a game stems from the loyalty one has to the principles underlying it. No matter what the opponents do to force a change in techniques used, the basic objectives must remain constant. To accomplish this, the following ideas are to be continuously activated:

1. Go Out and Get That Ball!

We will begin with a full-court defense, the kind best adapted to our personnel, and one with which all the players have been familiarized and trained to execute. We will try for the ball in the deep, back court, the three-quarter court or half-court. We plan to continue in the front court to attack aggressively the offense, making an effort to force a drastic

change in their game and to drive them into errors which will
yield the ball to us. When we get it, we will quickly and aggressively attack the optimum scoring area. We want that ball,
and we want to get it into that basket!

2. Get the Ball Off the Board!

If it takes three rebounders, four rebounders, or five, you
must *get the ball* if you plan to use the fast break from the defensive board. Failure here cuts down over half of your fast
break possibilities.

Against larger teams, we will use a rebound plan where the
entire team positions itself inside the three-second lane while
the ball is in flight after a field goal attempt. In other words,
we *zone the rebound* regardless of the defense we are otherwise using. Both guards are in the circle, one at the bottom of
the free-throw circle, the other just below the foul line. The
"inside" guard (the best rebounder) makes a try for all rebounds which rebound over the heads of the three players in
the rebound triangle. The "outside" guard goes for the long
rebound and also takes the outlet pass to either side of the
court (Diagram 154).

Diagram 154

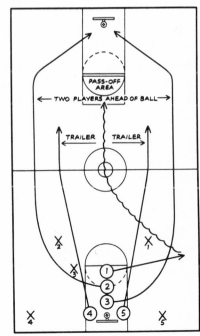

Against teams which do no have the height-size advantage, those which are more our size, we use the regular rebound triangle by our forwards and center, the guards follow up any offensive field-goal attempt to the top of the foul circle then immediately go to their next assignment (which is either receiving the outlet pass or taking an outside lane down court *fast!*).

We want the ball more than the defensive rebound and the made field-goal afford. We must employ harassing defenses to multiply our own offensive opportunities. Part of the fast break offense is an aggressive defense. *We must have that ball!*

3. Get it Out!

The position of the ball as it rebounds determines the side to which the outlet pass will be released. If it rebounds to the left or center (as you face the goal), the outlet pass receiver will take his receiving position along the left side-line. If it rebounds to the right, the outlet pass goes to the right side-line. The actual position of the receiver from corner base-line to mid-court is determined by the ability of the defensive rebounder, by the type of defense employed against the receiver, and by the size, strength, and aggressiveness of the offensive rebounders. There is an outlet-pass receiving position for every situation. The receiving guard *hustles every time* to receive this all-important pass. We use the station on the side line opposite the top of the circle most frequently. It seems to be the best position, all factors considered. (Our team considers a rebound as valid only when it is secured *and* immediately released to a receiver.) When a field goal or free throw is made, we use an offensive, right side-line station for the quick end-line throw-in by a designated rebounder.

4. Get Down Court!

Whenever interceptions, loose balls, recoveries, or steals are involved, we *quickly fill the three fast break lanes!* Our dribbler takes the center lane or ends up in the center lane by the time he reaches the pass-off area, which begins a few feet above the top of circle and extends to the foul line (Diagram 154). A similar procedure is followed on defensive rebounds after the field-goal attempt, after the free-throw attempt, and after the field-goal made and free-throw made. Get down, in front of the ball!

5. Fill the Three Lanes!

The center lane and the outside (side line) lanes must contain three players, two of whom are ahead of the ball or who are sprinting for such a position (Diagram 154).

The guard, other than the one who stations himself on the side line for the outlet pass, is the "guard going" each time he anticipates possession or each time possession of the ball is actually obtained. He speeds quickly down court, his primary function being to depress the defense (at least one defender usually goes with him). His secondary function is to receive the long pass, which is unlikely and seldom accomplished, but possible on occasions.

Only one of the guards may be particularly adapted to the outlet-pass receiving responsibilities. That is, only one may be able to handle the center lane. In that case, each guard will be assigned to do one thing—one will break each time, one will take the outlet pass each time. Needless to point out is the fact that the inability to interchange guard responsibilities places a serious limitation on the speed with which the fast break can be launched. Two good guards are invaluable.

The third lane is *the key lane*. It is this lane which gives the 3-on-2 situation. Of course, if the 2-on-1 or 3-on-1 situation arises, so much the better, but a team should strive for the 3-on-2 fast break since it gives an advantage over the defensive alignment of "2 back," which all teams strive for as a normal, defensive beginning against the fast break attack.

To put it another way, all teams plan to have two men in

the back court or prepared to get into the back court for defensive purposes. The fast break offense which succeeds most is one which can get *three* men into the optimum scoring area before *three* defensive men can get between them and the goal and organize themselves.

The fastest of the three defensive rebounders fills the third lane (or whoever of the three can fill this lane earliest after the rebounding chore has been taken care of). Under certain conditions, the third man may be a specifically assigned player; for instance, when his opponent is physically lacking in stamina and fails to run consistently to a defensive position, or when the offensive player is more skilled in the scoring department than his teammates.

6. Trailers, Follow Up!

In all of our fast break plans (with one exception) our rebounders go to the lane to which the outlet pass is thrown. In fact, they are to compete against each other in the first half of the full court to see which can be the third man on the fast break. The two rebounders who fail to become a part of the first three men down then move out of the third lane to fill lanes four and five. From lanes four and five, they will remain in the back court to protect against a return fast break, or follow through to the scoring area for the close shot, or rush the offensive board as a follow-up to the field goal attempt, or shoot as a trailer from the intermediate area.

7. Free Lance!

Look for opportunities to follow the initial stages of the fast break with free-lane moves which result in *a continued assault on the goal.* Utilize the period between the end of the fast break and the beginning of the secondary offense by taking advantage of defensive errors and misplacements which may occur as the defense reorganizes itself. (The defense is often busy trying to match up or re-form itself.) *Keep the pressure on!*

Move from the fast break, to free-lance, to set offense, with continuous, threatening maneuvers.

8. Fatigue is a Psychological Phenomenon!

Superior conditioning, achieved through cross-country running which precedes the season's opening by three to four weeks, is a *must*. Some games, we plan to beat teams with better players by running them into errors and misjudgments solely caused by fast-break-induced fatigue. Our team, however, cannot admit fatigue as a factor in their own performance. It is nonexistent as long as the desire to excel is uppermost in the player's mind. A player does not tire if he wants to win badly enough. Our conditioning objective is to have each player on the squad in such a state of physical readiness that he can play 40 minutes of full-court offense, combined with a full-court defense. When the player can manage this performance, he is ready for any game, since all other games are less demanding.

QUESTIONS AND ANSWERS

There are many questions often asked about the fast break system which I employ and about the fast break offense which others use successfully. A few of these follow:

1. *Q.* What does a fast-breaking team do at tournament time?
   A. Do not alter your game. Never slow a team down, except by substitutions. Go all out. The stronger a team is physically, the greater its powers of recuperation. There is nothing to fear in a tournament if your team is conditioned to play the fast break game. We must feel that the fast break team has the tournament advantage.

   During the fifth consecutive night of play in the 1958 National Association of Intercollegiate Athletics Championship Tournament, my team scored over 100 points against a seeded opponent in a game in which not a single substitution was made. In 1959, in another NAIA Championship Tournament on the *fourth* successive night of play my team played in another high-scoring battle (115–85) without a substitution being made until the final two or three minutes.

EACH PLAYER ON THE SQUAD MUST CONDITION HIMSELF AS IF THERE WOULD BE NO SUBSTITUTION IN HIS POSITION!

2. Q. What adjustments are made to the fast break against teams with superior height and size?

A. There must be a team, rebounding technique used which involves all five players. The outlet pass goes flat or parallel to the base line. The "four-second rule" is applied, in which I ask all five of our men to clear the back court in four seconds every time we get possession for "run 'em down" purposes. All phases of the fast break must be utilized fully. This will include the use of the "trailers" and their follow-up possibilities (Chapter 10).

Furthermore, you must begin your defense against the big team as soon as they gain possession of the ball. The kind of defense which picks them up all over the floor is one chance you have of decreasing height advantage.

3. Q. What is the reaction of a fast-breaking team to a team which withholds the ball from play?

A. The team must be trained to play a strong, aggressive, forcing defense to partially or fully offset the "control" tactics. The team must not relinquish its own attack and be influenced into playing the control team's game when it gets the ball. "*You* can't go when they've got it, but *they* must go when you get it."

4. Q. Which player should be the most "complete" player in the fast break offense? On which player do you spend the most coaching time?

A. The guard who best receives the outlet pass and dribbles the center lane should have the most all-around
talent. All other positions can be manned by "special-
ists" (good players in a limited way), who can do one
or two things well but who need not show great versatility.

5. Q. Does your team wear special shoes or lightweight uni-
forms in practice or games?

A. No. We found low-cut shoes made no appreciable difference, nor have we ever given up requiring two pairs
of socks to be worn at all times.

6. Q. How long does your team engage in a roadwork,
conditioning program?

A. Until the playing season begins and thereafter whenever signs of poor physical condition occur in an individual or in the team in general.

7. Q. Do you often miss good players because you insist on
the running game?

A. Once in a while, not often.

8. Q. What phases of the game require better than average
skill other than the center-lane dribble?

A. The option shot, pass-off, or controlled dribble or stop
by the driving, outside-lane player.

9. Q. Are you very strict on diet?

A. On days of the game, on trips, and during the tournaments, yes; otherwise, no. During a tournament we cut
down to two meals during the day and an after-game,
light lunch.

10. Q. What is the most important factor in the success of your
fast break system or any other fast break offense?

A. *Determination on the part of the players.* I have stated
before and will state again that the mechanics of the
fast break offense are simple, easily organized, easily
understood, and learned. The skills necessary for each
component are not the kind which will identify a player

as a "super-star." Talent is required, but the essential ingredient is the sheer *determination* to do the job assigned. In no other offense is there as much dependence on physical endurance, stamina, and just plan "guts" as there is in the full-court, fast break game. The *determination* to get the rebound and get it to the receiver; the *determination* to be in position to receive the outlet pass each and every time; the *determination* to outrun the opponents through the lanes to the 2-on-1, 3-on-2, 4-on-3, 5-on-4 advantage *each time* the team has the ball in its possession; the *determination* to play any type of defense which will increase the scoring opportunities, including the full-court, pressing defense. *This* is the element of success. Few offenses are so dependent on attitude for success. No other offense requires the player to face such hardships of continuous physical application. Along with the attitude of "wanting to win," there must be the accompanying *determination* to overcome the physical barriers to victory.

The fast break offense played "championship style" offers to the player one of basketball's greatest challenges. It has been my very good fortune to have found a few who could accept and meet it.

Index